SALAD

Edible

Series Editor: Andrew F. Smith

EDIBLE is a revolutionary series of books dedicated to food and drink that explores the rich history of cuisine. Each book reveals the global history and culture of one type of food or beverage.

Already published

Salad

A Global History

Judith Weinraub

REAKTION BOOKS

Published by Reaktion Books Ltd
Unit 32, Waterside
44–48 Wharf Road
London N1 7UX, UK
www.reaktionbooks.co.uk

First published 2016

Printed and bound in China by 1010 Printing International Ltd

A catalogue record for this book is available from the British Library

ISBN 978 1 78023 658 2

Contents

Introduction

In 1970, I left New York and moved to London for three years with my new husband. I'd travelled in Europe before then, but I'd never actually lived outside the United States, and I was relieved that my first full-time experience in a new country would be conducted in English. I was prepared for the possibility that the manners, politics, gender roles and even eating patterns might be a little different. (Everybody I knew had – incorrectly – warned me about English food.) But I hadn't fully anticipated the many cultural differences I'd encounter, or even that basic everyday foods might be a little off-kilter from what I was used to.

Like a salad or a sandwich.

Soon after we arrived on a flight that landed after most restaurants were closed for the evening, our hotel – an ageing *grande dame* near Victoria Station – took pity on the hungry young Americans and said they could provide chicken sandwiches. Salvation was at hand. But what soon came to the table were plates topped with two slim slices of buttered, crustless white bread enrobing paper-thin slivers of chicken, the whole business about half an inch thick. Not quite like the overstuffed sandwiches I was used to in American delis and restaurants! That said, what we were served at least bore a resemblance to what I thought of as a sandwich. Salads were another matter altogether. I was used to abundant bowls of greens, sometimes topped by strips of meats and cheese, a small can of tuna on a bed of iceberg lettuce, a plate of cottage cheese and fruit or even just a diminutive plate of greens decorated with strips of carrots and tomato wedges. On an early foray outside the hotel, I ordered a 'cold chicken salad' at a modest restaurant near the train station (the 'cold' part, not to mention the location, should have warned me off). When the 'chicken salad' arrived, it consisted of a dry, and indeed cold, roasted chicken leg and a few sad leaves of lettuce. A bottle of salad cream – a viscous liquid I'd never encountered before – stood nearby.

I was beginning to worry that those predictions about English food might be true. But I was wrong. I soon learned that a variety of adventurous, delicious salad concoctions were being made daily at the original Crank's, an upmarket 'health-food' hangout just off Carnaby Street, which was then the epicentre of all things cool. As a shopper and home cook, I marvelled at the excellent produce available, not only at Harrods Food Hall but at greengrocers all over the city, where I saw more local vegetables than I'd ever seen at a typical American supermarket – especially if you counted nearby Western Europe as local.

I soon saw that my chicken salad experience pointed out what I had kind of known but hadn't fully comprehended: that I couldn't assume a common language – or even the same word – would guarantee agreed-upon culinary definitions, even with something as seemingly straightforward as salad. Indeed, decades later, as I did the research for this book, I noticed that the word 'salad' (in various forms and languages) keeps coming up Zelig-like throughout food history – on menus, in ancient cookbooks, in descriptions

Mozzarella and tomato salad.

of banquets, in novels – sometimes with and at other times without qualifying descriptions. This was astonishing to me. Did everybody simply 'know' what salads were?

Indeed, the essential ingredients associated with European and American salads – the lettuces, the olive oil, the vinegar or lemon, the salt – are documented to have been around for centuries. (In countries outside that tradition – Northern Europe, Asia, parts of India and Africa — salad eating is more recent.) But how were these ingredients put together? What else might be in the salad? What role did salads play in an overall diet in different times, and for which social classes? How and when were they eaten? Were they eaten with forks or with fingers?

Research would show that although what is generally known as salad often includes some kind of greens and a dressing, the answers to these questions have varied with the times and venues. What was thought of as salad – *acetaria* in Latin, *insalata* in old Italian, *salade* in old French, sallet in English – at one time and place inevitably reflected specific eating patterns, cultural values, climates and agricultural realities, taste profiles and ideas about physiology, health and medicine. But the impulse to consume some kind of (usually) uncooked greens with a dressing has been reported for centuries. On top of uncooked greens, initially in more moneyed kitchens, a grab bag of other ingredients – roasted meats, offal, cheeses, herbs, bread – was piled, making it virtually impossible to provide a simple definition.

Dishes that have been called salads include wild herbs or cultivated leafy greens with a salted dressing; cold vegetable dishes designed to correct an imbalance within the body as set out by the theory of humours articulated by the prominent

Traditional healthy panzanella salad.

second-century physician and philosopher Galen; cresses, herbs and lettuces set alongside large roasted meats in Renaissance and post-Renaissance banquets; cold dishes with a kind of salad dressing that don't even contain vegetables except for a whisper of lettuce; ladylike dainties sometimes featuring vegetables, lobster or chicken, conjured up in early twentieth-century American kitchens; tidy side-dishes eaten alongside, before or after a meal; low-calorie plates designed to promote or maintain weight loss; and, at the opposite extreme, conglomerations of piled-on pasta or potato salads, canned beans, tuna salads, cooked and raw vegetables, fake crab and maybe some greens selected from a late twentieth-century salad bar; packaged bags of greens destined for the home salad bowl; Asian interpretations of the essentially Western European prototype; platforms for inventive chefs; even towers of vegetable foam. Salads have been individual courses in the sequence of a meal, side-dishes or, sometimes – especially in the late twentieth and early twenty-first centuries – the entire meal. They have been served before the main meal or after. Sometimes salads have been served in between courses as a holding pattern between hot courses or as a kind of palate refresher.

Because salads traditionally have either consisted of or included raw vegetables, they provide a contrast in heat, texture and flavour in the context of a meal. The salads made with cooked and cooled vegetables offer that contrast as well. (Although this book focuses primarily on the trajectory of the European salad tradition, dishes now described as salads have emerged in other parts of the world. They sometimes do and sometimes don't look like Western salads, and generally they don't rely on lettuces, but, like European and American salads, they provide a contrast in heat and texture to the main dishes in a meal, and when possible, they highlight local

Waldorf salad with walnuts, celery and apple on a bed of fresh lettuce.

vegetables – sometimes raw, sometimes cooked and cooled – and a dressing.)

Clearly the salad story is not straightforward, and the word has become almost impossible to define in a way that works for the many different dishes that have been and are called salads. That said, the story seems to be continuous. In one way or another, we have constructed salads by building on – and even sometimes by leaving out – the combination of leafy greens and dressings that were their original ingredients. And the way in which we did and continue to do that is not only 'culinary' but a mirror of and response to the demands and expectations of the local food cultures of the day.

I

In the Beginning there was Lettuce: Salad as Medicine

Many doctors judge this vegetable [lettuce] to be superior to all the other[s].

Galen of Pergamon, *On Food and Diet*, 2nd century

Was there ever a civilized world without salads? Praised by Greek poets, a regular accompaniment to roasted meats on Roman banquet tables, eagerly consumed by French royalty and taken for granted on today's family dinner tables, cafeteria trays, airline meals, salad bars and at farmers' markets and even fast-food outlets, salads of some sort have been part of eating patterns for centuries. Today salads are a standard part of our diet. We enjoy the range of ingredients we choose to put into them. We praise ourselves for consuming such a 'healthy' food. We take them for granted. But the story is not a simple one. Once the uncredited bit player in a belittled group of foods (vegetables), salads are now the versatile stars of contemporary eating. How did that happen?

In the beginning, long before there were mixed green salads and Caesar salads and bagged salads and bottled salad dressing and salad bars, there was only one generally respected vegetable: lettuce. Other vegetables were seen as having various properties that were potentially injurious to an assortment

The Caesar salad appears on hotel and restaurant menus all over the world.

of health conditions. But not lettuce. At least as far back as the Roman Empire, philosophers, essayists and historians valued lettuce – then the only vegetable that was regularly eaten raw. Today we might not recognize those lettuces of long ago. Unlike the iceberg or butterhead (Boston or Bibb) varieties of today, ancient lettuces were closer to today's romaine, but smaller and more bitter. Not mixed or tossed with other vegetables, lettuces were often accompanied by a salty dipping sauce, an ancestor of today's dressings.

Were they salads? They weren't called 'salads' – that wouldn't happen until after the appearance of the word *salade* centuries later, ultimately derived from the Latin *herba salata* or salted herbs. And they would have been consumed differently: instead of being served as a separate dish or course, salads were either presented among the many dishes at a grand meal, or as a complement to roasts. Since forks hadn't yet arrived on the scene, the lettuce leaves or similar greens, whether cultivated or wild, would have been dipped into the dressing.

The moneyed classes preferred cultivated lettuces. The ones eaten by the lower classes were mostly foraged or grown on small garden plots. But no matter where the lettuces came from, unlike other vegetables, they were eaten uncooked and accompanied by a mix of oil, *garum* (a kind of salty fermented fish sauce akin to contemporary soy sauce) and/or vinegar. In antiquity and for hundreds of years afterwards, such salads didn't have the standing of a separate course. But there they were, providing a contrast to the heat, textures and flavours of the cooked foods in a meal, just as salads often do today.

However those lettuces were grown and consumed, the aristocrats who ate them and the cooks who prepared them were aware of the status accorded the vegetable because of its presumed medical properties. 'It is clear', said the learned Galen of Pergamon, 'that of all the foods, this is the one with the best juices. And if in fact it does have in its nature to produce a lot of blood, it does not give rise to any other humours.'

Romaine, a popular lettuce for salads, available at most supermarkets and grocery stores.

Boiled egg on a traditional *salade Lyonnaise*.

Detail of a salad in an anonymous early 17th-century *Supper at Emmaus*.

Blood? Humours? To contemporary readers, Galen's non-culinary observations and conclusions about lettuce are mystifying, but in antiquity, they were logical extensions of medical theory. Today we look at foods individually rather than as part of a complicated dietary, medical, physiological and philosophical system. But in the ancient world, before the complexities of body mechanics were understood, foods weren't thought of simply as foods. Instead, individual foods were seen as components in the theory of the four humours – then the reigning explanation about how the body works.

Accepted as a kind of medicine, humoral theory was a physiological and philosophical system originally laid out by the ancient Greek physician Hippocrates, but codified two centuries later by Galen. Galenic medicine looked at the body as a balance – or more commonly, an imbalance – of the four bodily fluids (humours): black bile, yellow bile, phlegm and blood. Each of these fluids was characterized by varying degrees of hot, cold, warm and dry properties and had a corresponding temperament – sanguine, phlegmatic, choleric and melancholic – which were characterized by which humour predominated. Each food comprised a combination of these qualities. Making things even more complicated, within that system each person was thought to have a particular combination of the four elements. What was ingested and how it was cooked would alter the balance of humours in the body – often adversely. However, a balanced diet (according to the humours) could realign an unbalanced body and help to keep it that way. Welcome to the dietary theory of the ancient world.

Much of what we know about the foods of Greek and Roman antiquity comes from Galen, a prolific writer and thinker. Not part of the aristocracy, his family was nevertheless wealthy and influential. His father was a doctor – then not considered a particularly high-class occupation. Even so, when one night he dreamed that his then seventeen-year-old son should also become a doctor, Galen accepted the omen. His education was broad, embracing mathematics and philosophy as well as the more standard rhetoric and literature. A wide-ranging reader, he was influenced heavily by Hippocrates' ideas about diet and health, and he travelled widely to study and learn from the experts and to conduct his own research. A stint as a doctor at a gladiatorial school in Pergamon, where doctors were encouraged to repair injured bodies, taught him anatomy. It also gave him the opportunity to experiment with changes in diet to see how eating different foods could help rebuild the strength of the injured gladiators.

One of Galen's treatises, *On the Power of Foods*, is a kitchen window onto the dietary theory and eating habits of the Roman Empire, from the tables of the wealthy to the make-do habits of the poor. Cataloguing all the known foods into categories such as fruits, vegetables, grains, fish, poultry, meats, offal and dairy products, Galen classified them according to their tastes, digestive properties and humoral effects. Did they promote one or another of the humours? Were they good or bad for the stomach? Did they pass through the body quickly? Were they difficult or easy to digest? He also described how they were generally cooked and served and even provided a few recipes. When viewed that way, lettuce occupied a special place among vegetables. Galen's admiration for it is notable. So is his observation that for the most part, lettuce was eaten raw with a kind of dressing of olive oil, *garum* and vinegar – in other words, not all that different from today's green salads.

Despite the medical thinking of the time that warned against eating raw fruits and vegetables because of their 'cold' nature, Galen singled out lettuce as the food with the 'best juices'. Infuriatingly, however, instead of describing it precisely, he referred to it as 'what everyone today calls lettuce'. Everyone, that is, who belonged to the upper classes and either grew lettuce on their country estates or could afford to buy it in town – and perhaps also the families who worked on farms, but had small market gardens of their own. Apparently, not everyone prized lettuce as much as Galen, who defended it in both medical and matter-of-fact terms. 'If a considerable amount of blood is alleged to collect as a result of lettuces, and this is why they are censured,' he says, 'it is extremely easy to correct the defect since those who eat them can first engage in more exercise, and second, eat fewer of them.'

According to Galen, lettuce – sometimes raw, sometimes cooked – could help restore bodily balance and health, and often in rather specific ways. When he began having health problems with his teeth, for example, Galen found it helpful to eat lettuce (before it began to flower and seed) that had first been boiled in water. And eaten in the evening, he confided, lettuce was the only remedy for his insomnia. His admiration for raw lettuce is markedly different from his views on the other vegetables available in the ancient world that we think of as natural inclusions in salads today. Those he either disparaged, or described the non-salad-like ways (that is, cooked) in which they were eaten.

Writing about endives and chicory, for example, he found their medical properties almost as powerful as lettuce, but their taste inferior. Beetroot, he said, had little nourishment, 'as is the case with other vegetables, but eaten with mustard or at least with vinegar,' he wrote, 'they are a good medicine for those with complaints of the spleen'. 'In fact, you could quite reasonably call beetroot a medicine rather than a food.' Carrots, like other roots, were thought of as diuretics, yet, according to Galen, were difficult to digest. Cucumbers weren't favoured because of 'a wretched juice' that caused malignant fevers and could collect unnoticed in the veins over time. Radishes – really a root rather than a vegetable – could also be eaten raw, as a starter with fish sauce, to relax the bowels, he explained, observing that some people poured vinegar over them, and that country people served them with bread. Fennel he included in a group of plants that he said people boil and eat when forced to in times of food shortage. Rocket (arugula) was better eaten with lettuce leaves rather than on its own, when, he observed, it could cause headaches. As for onions, garlic and leeks, he said that on the whole they shouldn't be served until they were cooked, and that boiling them two or three times could take away their harshness.

Discussing the way vegetables were eaten, Galen reported that they were often twice-cooked – once partially in boiling water, then drained and cooked again until tender – or, like artichokes, thoroughly boiled and served with olive oil, fish sauce or wine. Lettuce, however, had a different culinary history. By Galen's time, it was clear that the habit of eating raw lettuce with some kind of dressing had been around for some time, though in all likelihood it was not regularly enjoyed by all classes of society. Lettuces of some sort appear to have been

James Gillray, *Temperance Enjoying a Frugal Meal*, 1792.

around throughout antiquity, when they were put to a variety of uses: as an aphrodisiac in Egypt, as a sedative in Greece and as a dampener of the sex drive in ancient Rome.

The first-century poet Martial writes of a variety of uses, including a medicinal one when he writes: 'Eat lettuce and soft apples eat: For you, Phoebus, have the harsh face of a defecating man.' For culinary purposes, he also suggested that lettuce should be eaten at the beginning of a feast. And when inviting a guest to dinner, he included on the menu an enticement that seems very much like a modern tuna salad: sliced leeks, wholesome lettuce and tunny (tuna) with rue and the sauce of an egg. In the first century Pliny the Elder wrote that the Greeks distinguished three varieties of lettuce: a long, stalked one, a herbaceous, green one and a low, squat one. But he also mentioned garden lettuce and noted that it was green. Pliny described lettuces as *acetaria* – garden produce that 'needs no fire and ensures economy in fuel' and is 'always ready and at hand'.

How much attention did eaters in the ancient world give to such 'medical' or philosophical analyses of lettuce and other greens? We don't know. But theory, whether medical, culinary or philosophical, is a funny thing. It rarely informs us about what was actually eaten, and it's just not realistic to conclude that Galenic medical precepts governed all dietary choices. In the real world people ate what was available, what they could afford to eat and, to the extent to which it was possible, what they liked. Therefore all discussion of salads, and for that matter all the recipes of that era that have been handed down to us, reflect the habits and preferences of the ruling classes, who, unlike workers, slaves and freed men, could choose what they ate.

Romans preferred farm-raised or greenhouse-grown foods to foods foraged from the wild. For the lower classes

A slaw of cabbages can be more filling than a green salad.

(slaves and labourers), especially those who lived in cities, lettuces and other cultivated greens would have been a costly extra, and certainly not the kind of food one could fill up on. They would have had to forage, occasionally manage to afford what was in season, or do without. In any case they were not likely to be bogged down in philosophical considerations of vegetables. The higher economic classes could afford to buy the ingredients they wanted – and to consider the medical implications of lettuce and other leafy greens. Another factor regarding salads, which today are generally considered in the context of a meal, is that today's meals have a more predictable structure than those in antiquity that varied according to class, geographical location and availability. Contemporary eating habits presuppose breakfasts, lunches and dinners, a pattern that only became established after the Industrial Revolution.

Happily, there is another ancient source for real-life examples: *De re coquinaria* (The Art of Cooking). The oldest collection of European recipes to survive, *De re coquinaria* reflects what the moneyed classes were actually served. Its author is said to be one Marcus Gavius Apicius, a wealthy early first-century Roman epicure. Apicius is said to have thrown drunken, over-the-top banquets and orgies and to have taken his own life when he feared he was running out of money for luxurious banquets, yet little is known about him for certain. The book's almost 500 upmarket, often complicated recipes were assembled, then divided into ten books, and organized in much the same manner as a contemporary cookbook. They include garde manger (room temperature) preparations, meat, poultry, vegetables, pulses, seafood and luxury dishes. The recipes were in all likelihood those of professional chefs working for families wealthy enough to have cooks in the first place – in other words, a collection for the better-off population.

Cottage cheese salad with pineapple and strawberries on a bed of lettuce.

The recipes are now thought to have been put together by multiple cooks over time, rather than solely by Apicius, and were initially written for other cooks. Originally associated with gluttony, many of the recipes would have been costly to prepare and were clearly created for the financially comfortable classes whose kitchen workers or cooks could afford the ingredients they needed, including fresh, or greenhouse-fresh, vegetables. What we would call salads could be simple or relatively complex, with many non-vegetal ingredients – a two-pronged approach to salads that has continued ever since, confusing any attempt at a simple definition of the word 'salad'.

Although the recipes in *De re coquinaria* are not the stuff of everyday eating, the absence of more basic recipes doesn't mean that they weren't regularly consumed. The cooks preparing vegetable dishes such as an hors-d'oeuvre of parboiled gourds stuffed with pepper, lovage, oregano, the ever-present *garum*, cooked brains and eggs all tied up and fried, and then served with a sauce, would certainly first have had to show proficiency at preparing basic dishes like dressed lettuces or greens.

Many raw vegetables that we think of as salad-friendly – greens, celery, parsley, fresh coriander, fresh sorrel – were included in a few recipes for what we might recognize as an ancient salad, such as rustic greens, endive or lettuce with *garum*, oil and vinegar. But the belief that vegetables in general were better for the body when cooked rather than raw was still in operation. So there are many more recipes based on cooked vegetables, such as a dish of mashed, finely chopped celery with pepper, lovage, oregano, onion wine, garum and oil, all cooked in a pan. Three other recipes called *sala cattabia*, layered compound dishes of bread, cheese, some cooked vegetables, herbs, chicken and a dressing, are thought by scholars to be salads, and in any case were served cold. Concoctions that are more like the complicated salmagundi salads of the eighteenth century than simple greens with dressing, these dishes are heavily laden not only with herbs but with honey, vinegar, fermented fish sauces, cheeses, cucumbers, onions, softened bread, garlic, chicken and even spiced wine.

Consider the instructions for a *sala cattabia* in the style of Apicius – in a way, a very elaborate chicken salad:

> Put in a mortar celery seed, dry pennyroyal, dry mint, ginger, green coriander, de-seeded raisins, honey, vinegar, oil and wine. Pound together. Put in a small pot pieces of Picentine bread [light spongy semolina bread] interlayered with cooked chicken meat, goats' sweetbreads, Vestine cheese, pine nuts, cucumber, finely chopped dried onions. Pour the sauce over [the ingredients]; stand [the pot] in snow for an hour, sprinkle with pepper and serve.

Recipes that rich with undoubtedly expensive ingredients are likely to have vanished with the end of the Roman Empire. But the conviction that foods and the way they were cooked and served had medicinal implications did not. And amazingly, that belief – even with salads – was still around many centuries later.

2
Salads Catch On

Saturday I went to the tavern: salad and omelette, and cheese, and
I felt good.

Jacopo Pontormo, diary, 1554

By the spring of 1554, when the Renaissance painter Jacopo
Pontormo filled his diary with descriptions of the foods he
enjoyed, salads were emerging from a bumpy few centuries.
During the Middle Ages, with its wars, decimating plagues
and famine, salads – either greens and a dressing or more
elaborate cold vegetable dishes – hadn't been particularly
sought-after. And when they did appear, they emerged primarily on the tables of the wealthy. Moreover, vegetables still
weren't valued in the way they are today. No other theory had
emerged to supplant Galen's wariness of raw vegetables, or
his belief that human health depended on the correct balance
of the four humours within the body. And any notion of
today's understanding of the specific health properties of
fruits and vegetables was still a long way in the future.

That said, the impact of Galen's thinking emerged again
after the Middle Ages, first during the Renaissance revival
with its appreciation of classical texts – nutritional and
culinary as well as literary – and even more so after Johannes

Gutenberg's invention of the printing press in 1440 made the ancient medical and culinary texts (including Apicius in Latin) available to a wider world.

Without any dietary or medical theory successfully challenging Galen, let alone any understanding of how the body actually worked, the ancient distrust of vegetables and fruit – and by extension, salads – continued well into the seventeenth and even the eighteenth centuries. (So did the popular idea that vegetables were peasant food more fit for animals than people.) Galenic theorists of the time considered fruits and vegetables putrefying and continued to recommend that they be used sparingly, although some individual ones were thought to help balance some unbalanced bodies. That said, everyday reality rarely abides by theoretical constructs, and gradually the idea of eating according to 'medical' precepts was starting to weaken.

Early Salads in Italy

Food historians think that salad-like foods have been eaten in Italy for a very long time. By the sixteenth century, as evidenced by Pontormo's eating habits (many salads, roasted meats, bread, almonds, walnuts and eggs), salads had become a more common component of Italian upper-class eating. At that time meals that included salads – whether mixed greens or the more complicated high-fashion assemblages of antiquity – would have continued to be an option only for the wealthy, who often cared about the spectacle of the foods on their tables and how that reflected societal rank more than they did about 'science' or medicine. On the opposite end of the economic scale, ordinary people lived in a real world with cultural and economic strictures and less ability – or even desire – to worry how salad vegetables ranked on the hot/ dry, cold/wet scale, and therefore ate what they could afford to buy or grow.

Geography and climate were important dietary factors too. Salad vegetables or leafy greens are more likely to grow in a welcoming climate. So it's no surprise that salads took hold earlier in Italy, where a family with even a tiny bit of land could grow a few vegetables, than they did in the rest of Europe. Fortunately for food history, some Italian writers embraced the opportunity to record the foods of the time (including salads), and the way each should be cooked and eaten. Their writings show that salads – at least greens and a dressing – were catching on in Italy, defying the low esteem accorded to vegetables.

The very first cookbook ever printed, the 1474 *De honesta voluptate et valetudine* (On Right Pleasure and Good Health), was written by the humanist scholar Bartolomeo Sacchi, better known today as Platina. As an intellectual starting point, his writings still relied on the ancient humoral theory that had been codified by Galen. But the goal was different and reflected the attitudes of aristocrats in the second half of the fifteenth century and how they could live in an agreeable and healthy manner. As well as providing recipes, Platina discussed how to choose a place to live, how to set a table and what to eat at the start of a meal, as well as including observations on exercise, sleep and sexual activity. He commented on the foods and condiments of his time and described the order in which foods should be served, including, for example, the medical suggestion that laxative foods, including leafy greens and any- thing eaten raw with olive oil and vinegar, should be eaten first. Basic salads, or even fancier versions, were likely to be among the first dishes served at a meal anyway, he pointed out, according to the logic that dictated that cooler uncooked foods, which could stimulate the appetite, should be served before cooked ones.

Platina's recipes were adapted from the *Libri de arte coquinara*, written by the renowned contemporary chef Maestro Martino de Rossi. The result was an approach that paid homage to humoral doctrine in attitude, but reflected what the Roman elite actually ate. The book's many reprintings spread Platina's ideas throughout Western Europe. Some of the comments on foods echo Galen directly – consider Platina's approach to our old friend lettuce, which he, like Galen, valued for non-culinary reasons: 'They say the divine Augustus was preserved in a time of ill health by the use of lettuce, and no wonder, because it aids digestion and generates better blood than other vegetables.' His recipe for seasoned lettuce continues: 'Put in a dish, sprinkle with ground salt, pour in a little oil and more vinegar, and eat at once. Some add a little mint and parsley to it for seasoning, so that it does not seem entirely bland and the excessive chill of the lettuce does not harm the stomach.'

Such straightforward approaches to salads, as well as even more rudimentary ones, were rarely found in recipe books. The writers of long ago understood that cooks didn't need recipes to assemble simple salads. That said, when it came to more complicated salads, Platina's instructions were more precise:

There may be likewise a seasoned salad from lettuce, borage, mint, calamint, fennel, parsley, wild thyme, marjoram, chervil, sow-thistle, which doctors call tarazicon, lancet, which they call lamb's tongue, nightshade, flower of fennel, and several other aromatic herbs, well-washed and with the water pressed out. They need a large dish. They ought to be sprinkled with a lot of salt and

Melozo da Forin, *Pope Sixtus IV appoints Bartolomeo Platina Prefect of the Vatican Library*, c. 1477.

> moistened with oil, then after vinegar has been poured over and [the leaves and herbs] have sat for a little while, [more] oil is added and vinegar sprinkled on top.

Lest any eater simply chomp away too quickly, Platina included this warning: 'Their wild toughness demands eating and chewing well with the teeth.'

A century later, in 1570, the Renaissance chef Bartolomeo Scappi included many references to salad among the more than 1,000 recipes in his massive *Opera*, but few actual recipes for them. Instead, Scappi, who became the private cook to Pope Pius V, gave guidelines for preparing both raw and cooked vegetables for salads, among them asparagus, cucumber, spring onions, endive and green beans, as well as less predictable ingredients such as citron flowers, veal, goats' feet, hard-boiled eggs, macaroni, capers and currants. His examples of menus also refer to salad-like preparations – fresh sweet fennel, cooked artichokes with vinegar and salt, lettuce with borage flowers, salad with cucumber and spring onions. As he saw it, salads could include both cooked and raw vegetables, such as asparagus, endive, fennel, green beans and cucumber.

Scappi's *Opera* is particularly notable for its illustrative plates. One of them includes a set of dining implements including a new utensil, the fork – an implement essential to salad eating today and probably transformative then. In the grand homes where Scappi's recipes would have been used, the inclusion of the fork (as well as the more common knife and spoon) indicates that it was becoming a feature of aristocratic dining in Italy. (The fork appeared in Italy before the rest of Europe. In England, the earliest known mention of the fork comes from Thomas Coryate's *Crudities* in 1611. Coryate, a daring sort of eccentric, had taken a trip across parts of Europe in 1608, and on that journey he encountered an eating implement new to him: the fork. 'The Italians and also most strangers that are commorant in Italy do alwayes at their meals use a little forke, when they cut their meat', he wrote.)

Since vegetables were enjoyed more in sunny Italy than in other parts of Europe, a variety of salads emerged there early on. An Italian salad of the time might include lettuce as well as other greens and herbs that grew well there, such

The fork is an essential tool for eating salad.

as endive, chicory, watercress, burnet, tarragon and rocket, dressed with oil and vinegar, but there were also many other possible combinations.

Seventeenth-century Salads in England and France

The memories of those Italian salads haunted Giacomo Castelvetro, who, exiled for his religious beliefs, had taken up residence across the continent in meat-loving England. In his *The Fruits and Vegetables of Italy* of 1614, he described all the known fruits and vegetables eaten there, season by season, suggested how to prepare them and also specified the correct way to assemble salads. He stressed what is certainly an upper-class approach to preparing a salad. 'It takes more than good ingredients to make a salad, for success depends above all on knowing how to prepare them', he said, stressing the importance of washing salad greens several times to eliminate grit, shaking them well and then drying them with a clean linen cloth before even thinking of dressing them. That taken care of, his guidance for dressing a salad became the standard for centuries to come: 'Salads must be well salted with little vinegar and lots of oil.'

Castelvetro, whose writings make it clear that Galen's view of vegetables still held sway, particularly liked spring salads. 'It is barely possible to describe our delight in the delicious, gracious and wholesome green salads of this joyful season, I think for two reasons', he wrote: 'firstly because

Etching of woman buying salad vegetables by Bartolomeo Pinelli (1781–1835).

the cooked salads we ate in winter now seem so boring, and secondly because all this fresh greenery is such a pleasure to the eye, and a treat for the palate, and above all, a really important contribution to our health, purging us of all the melancholy and unwholesome humours accumulated during the drear winter months.'

But it wasn't only Italians who sought out salad in meat-loving England. The plagues, poverty and warfare of the Tudor and Elizabethan periods were not a time of agricultural plenty, but the wealthy always had food on their tables. And even though large cuts of meat were what people wanted to eat, somehow salads survived as a part of English high-class eating, and were seen on some English menus of the time. In cookbooks of the era as well, there are recipes for simple salads – mostly based on an assortment of greens, such as purslane, borage and orach, and herbs such as sage, hyssop and a kind of oregano – and for compound salads which married many diverse ingredients, often including a layer of greens.

In 1615, Gervase Markham, a writer, poet and horseman, provided a few recipes for both kinds of salads in his house-keeping and husbandry manual *The English Huswife*. Markham included recipes for boiled salads, preserved salads and pickled salads as well as strange salads – sometimes salad centrepieces not even meant for eating. Even the simple salads he described went far beyond the basics, including onions, chives, spring onions (scallions), radish roots, boiled carrots, turnips and also young lettuce, cabbage, purslane and other herbs, served with a little vinegar and oil and flavoured in the medieval style, with sugar.

By 1660, the Elizabethan-era chef Robert May included a chapter on 'sallets' in his cookbook, *The Accomplisht Cook*. They were far from simple. The first salad recipe he provides is a 'grand Sallet of divers Compounds' and includes small slices of cold roast capon or other roast meats mixed with minced tarragon and an onion, minced lettuce, capers, olives, pickled broom buds, mushrooms, oysters, lemon, orange, raisins, nuts, figs, potato, peas, oil and vinegar, all beautifully arranged. The other seventeen salad recipes don't include meats or fish, but they do include a variety of pickled vegetables as well as orange and lemon slices, raisins, beetroot, cucumbers, herbs and flowers.

In France, too, salads had become popular. Louis xiv loved salads, although he apparently refused to use a fork to eat them. Salads began to appear in dictionaries and

Niçoise salads, with tuna, egg, potato, olives, beans, cucumber and tomato, are popular all over the world.

'The Giant Gargantua Eats Six Pilgrims in a Salad', illustration by Gustave Doré from François Rabelais, *The Life of Gargantua and of Pantagruel* (1873 edition).

cookbooks of the time too. According to the late French historian Jean-Louis Flandrin in his *Arranging the Meal*, a *salade* was 'usually composed of raw greens, seasoned with salt, oil and vinegar'.

Relatively simple salads had begun to be so popular that they were reflected in French literature. Even in the sixteenth century, the writer François Rabelais had written of many salads, and in his *The Life of Gargantua and of Pantagruel*, he referred to a salad of lettuce, oil, vinegar and salt prepared by the giant Gargantua. (As it happens, Gargantua accidentally also ingested some pilgrims who had wandered their way into the huge salad.)

Although the ability to pay for the ingredients continued to be an issue, and fresh vegetables are rarely in the budgets of the poor, in Italy salads were not just for aristocrats. We may not know exactly how popular they were, but Jacopo Pontormo's diary indicates that salads were not only accompaniments to roasts at banquets. As part of his food diary, Pontormo listed salads of lettuce, goat's beard, capers, borage – even a cooked salad. Sometimes he simply referred to 'a salad' – presumably a standard food item that scholars today think meant fresh, salted, raw vegetables. As the diary attests, Pontormo sometimes ate them at the start of his meal, and sometimes as an integral part of his meals. Indeed, through the seventeenth century, the idea that salads would excite the appetite would linger. And so did arguments about when salads should be served – as a first course, as a last course, as accompaniments to roasts, or as side-dishes.

The Salad Eaters: Salvatore Massonio and John Evelyn

The most articulate and writerly defenders of salad eating spanned the century, and were of another order altogether. The Italian Salvatore Massonio (1550–1629) and the Englishman John Evelyn (1620–1706) would make it clear that salads had come of age.

Massonio was a physician, writer and passionate salad eater. In Italy, only half a century after Scappi's massive *Opera* had paid little attention to salads, Massonio devoted a book-length treatise to them. His *Archidipno: Salad and its Uses* (1627) reflects the appreciation and enjoyment that green vegetables had in Italy, where, Massonio claimed, salads, if not eaten by everyone, were well-known.

The unusual title was significant. *Archidipno* was a made-up word with Greek roots: *archi* (to start) and *diepnon* (dinner), indicating that salads at that time were (or should be) served as a first course – although the book acknowledges that some put salads on the table at the start of the meal and left them there. Reflecting the scientific understanding of the time, *Archidipno* expounded on the nature of salads, the ingredients that go into them and the author's thoughts on the nature and uses of an array of vegetables.

Massonio pointed out that all the components of salad are nourishing but, crediting Galen, he said that they have to be eaten in the right proportion, quality and quantity. He also considered issues such as whether eating salad increases the appetite, the conviction that salads don't go well with wine, and the idea that a waiting period before eating salads may be necessary, depending on what has already been eaten. Scholarly and replete with ancient sources, *Archidipno* dates salad eating as far back as the Trojans, when in Book x of the *Iliad*, Ulysses comes back to camp with a stag on his shoulders and is fed a meal that includes herbs dressed with oil and vinegar.

The primary content of *Archidipno* is made up of learned disquisitions on a lengthy range of individual ingredients and how to assemble them. Massonio begins with comments on the components of the dressing: vinegar (it has, he says 'the power to counteract venom'), olive oil ('treasured by the ancients') and salt, the ingredient so important that the word 'salad' has its roots in *sol*, the Latin word for salt. Pepper, he said, could 'gracefully season' salads and salt could turn a piece of chicken into a salad.

His list of salad ingredients is long, including predictable ones such as lettuce, cabbage and cucumber as well as many others – ramps, sprouts, fennel, rocket, edible flowers, fresh

Detail from Paolo Veronese, *The Wedding at Cana*, 1563.

herbs – that were grown in market gardens or the hothouses of the time, but were virtually unavailable in shops in Britain and North America until the late twentieth century. Most discussions of individual vegetables are accompanied, if not exactly by recipes, then by instructions for presenting them in salads. Among them are squash salad with various dressings; herbs and capers with cold pheasant, salted meat and tongue, apples and onions; radish salad; asparagus salad; cucumber salad; and, of course lettuce, here with lemon, anchovies, raisins and tuna. As for dressings, not surprisingly, Massonio wrote that 'The ordinary seasoning of the salad is vinegar, oil and salt and . . . he who eats it without the dressing . . . loses the point of its name.'

Some seventy years later, stressing harmony and balance, Massonio's English counterpart John Evelyn took salads to a new level in his extraordinary *Acetaria: A Discourse of Sallets*

Bottles of oil and vinegar.

of 1699. In it Evelyn defined salads – 'a particular composition of certain crude and fresh herbs, such as usually are, or may safely be eaten with some acetous juice, oyl, salt' – and praised them. An English country gentleman, Evelyn was also a diarist and scholar, a translator of French gardening texts and a founding member of the Royal Society. Always interested in horticulture as well as in food and health, he was passionate about gardens, sculpture and architecture. Before he wrote *Acetaria* (the term is Pliny the Elder's) late in his life, possibly to help plan and reconstruct the kitchen garden of his brother's estate, Wotton House, in Surrey, John Evelyn was best-known for *Sylva; or, A Discourse of Forest Trees*. During much of the English Civil War, Evelyn spent considerable time in the Netherlands, France and Italy. A gardener by inclination, he observed many plantings there – edible and otherwise – that were new to him. He also translated a French horticultural manual and a Latin garden poem, and was certainly familiar with the writings of Louis xiv's head gardener Jean-Baptiste de la Quintinie, so by the time he wrote *Acetaria*, Evelyn was aware of contemporaneous European plants and garden practices.

In his writing, Evelyn still referred to the wet/dry, hot/cold qualities of individual foods established by Galen, but he also rejoiced in the more earth-bound possibilities of vegetables, 'improved', he wrote, 'by culture, industry, and [the] art of the gardener'. That was new – even modern. As Evelyn saw it, mankind could have, and already had had, an influence on the quality and nature of vegetables.

Like Massonio, he provided an erudite and lengthy list of salad ingredients and dressing that seems to embody a mission: in addition to foods well-known in England, he was introducing some of the new fruits and vegetables he had observed and eaten during his European tour. Evelyn also

provided recipes and guidelines for salad making: clean
and drain your salad greens, remove damaged leaves, use the
best wine vinegar. His lengthy instructions for making salad
dressing advises the use of olive oil, vinegar and other liquid
acids, salt, mustard, pepper and the hard-boiled yolks of newly
laid eggs. He also shared his observations on how the ingredients were served in Europe, the best knives (silver) and which
serving dishes to use (porcelain, not too deep or too shallow),
when salads should be eaten, the effect of diet on the eater
and the virtues of vegetarianism.

Acetaria and the earlier *Archidipno* are amazingly modern
documents that give the reader a glimpse of both culinary
agriculture and salads of their times. Still, each treatise accepted
Galenic theory with regard to the health properties of foods,
although *Acetaria* less so. By the time Evelyn wrote *Acetaria*, he
was aware of contemporaneous European plants and garden
practices.

If Massonio tallied up the many salads and salad foods
eaten in Italy in the first quarter of the seventeenth century,
fifty years later Evelyn went even farther. He praised salad
foods that were already being eaten in England as well as those
more foreign foods that he thought could and by extension
should (for both culinary and health purposes) be eaten –
like broccoli from Naples, the dandelion roots he had seen
in the French countryside, the garlic enjoyed by Spaniards
and Italians, Spanish onions and, of course, lettuce. 'Lettuce', he wrote, 'ever was, and still continues the principal
foundation of the universal tribe of sallets: which is to cool
and refresh.'

By the century's end, classical health considerations
according to the theory of humours were losing their hold.
A new era was beckoning and with it a larger variety of culinary possibilities. There would still be the normal constraints

on eating patterns – the accessibility and affordability of ingredients as well as taste preferences. But a change was in the air. Salads, whether French, Italian, English or Spanish, would be free to be salads – reflections of the developing culinary traditions where they were assembled, served and eaten.

3
European and American Salads: Plain and Not So Plain

Then came the salad. I recommend it to those who have
confidence in me. It refreshes without weakening, and comforts
without irritating . . . it makes me younger.
Jean-Anthelme Brillat-Savarin, *The Physiology of Taste* (1825)

No longer weighed down by philosophical and medical bag-
gage, salad became a dish eaten by choice – and a desirable
one. Undoubtedly, the growing popularity of the fork in the
seventeenth century helped. Even so, faced with hundreds of
years of underlying disapproval of raw vegetables even as late
as the nineteenth century, except in Italy, salads in Europe
were not always embraced – perhaps a reason for Brillat-
Savarin's endorsement. Salad composition varied from country
to country and region to region. Some adhered mostly to a
plain greens, oil and vinegar identity. Others were packed
with many non-vegetal ingredients, creating not so plain
dishes that emerged out of local food cultures. The place that
salads should have in the order of a meal (first or last course)
was still an unsettled question.

Britain

In Britain, more or less plain salads turned up on both high and low tables. By the late seventeenth century, English upper-class eating embraced so-called 'grand sallets' – room-temperature vegetable dishes that bore no resemblance to simple greens and a dressing. Often composed of many ingredients in what must have been daunting combinations to a diner, grand salads included types of pickle, sauced meats and coloured jellies, creating dishes that certainly could have been meals in themselves. These assemblages, such as the ones described by the poet and writer Gervase Markham, and some of the complicated 'sallet' recipes in Robert May's *The Accomplisht Cook*, must have been sights to behold, a challenge to eat and expensive to assemble. The more straightforward possibilities enthusiastically recommended by John Evelyn in *Acetaria* would have been enjoyed by anyone who could afford the ingredients, or lived in an agricultural setting.

Both salad traditions continued in the eighteenth and nineteenth centuries. In England, some of the compound salads were known as salmagundi or salamongundy. The British cookery writer Hannah Glasse provided several recipes for them in *The Art of Cookery Made Plain and Easy* (1747), saying 'you may always make a Salamongundy of such things as you have, according to your fancy.' Those ingredients could include finely sliced lettuces or cabbages, chicken slices (white meat) or pieces (dark meat), boned anchovies, hard-boiled eggs, pickled onions, chopped parsley and an oil and vinegar dressing.

Plainer green salads had become so much a part of ordinary eating that casual references to salads in literature required no particular explanation. In the genteel world of *Pride and Prejudice*, set in the early nineteenth century, Jane

Austen mentioned dressing salad and a cucumber. Just plain lettuce might have seemed a bit sparse – cucumbers would have added crunch, and of course tomatoes had not yet gained acceptance, especially uncooked tomatoes.

That same year the Revd Sydney Smith, a scholar, Episcopal curate and popular lecturer, was enjoying country living when he created a rhyming recipe expressing an enthusiasm for salads and salad dressings. The poetic dressing for a winter salad included salt, oil, vinegar, mustard, egg yolk, onion and anchovy sauce, and reflects the pleasure that the English moneyed class took in a well-dressed salad. (See pp. 106–7 for the complete recipe.) The last two lines of the recipe point to a definite upgrade in status:

> Then though green turtle fail, though venison's tough
> And ham and turkey are not boiled enough,
> Serenely full, the Epicure may say –
> Fate cannot harm me, I have dined today.

In other words, a salad with this dressing would be so satisfying and delightful that it could make amends for a not particularly well prepared ham or turkey.

Seventy years later and many miles away, in America just after the Civil War, the humorist and writer Frederick Swartwout Cozzens created a 'learned' character – one Dr Bushwhacker – who had opinions on many foods, including lettuce and salads. Echoing the Revd Smith, Dr Bushwhacker repeated a version of the recipe to his friends, and also spoke of – what else? – lettuce as the almost inevitable base. '*Lactuca*, or lettuce, is one of the most common vegetables in the world', he wrote. 'It has been known, sire, from time immemorial, it was common on the tables of the ancients, as it is now, and was eaten in the same way, sir, dressed with oil and vinegar.'

France

In France, it was a different story. In the seventeenth century, a culinary revolution had taken place, and salads had little place in it. Articulated by *Le Cuisinier françois*, a 1651 cookbook and gastronomic guide by François Pierre de la Varenne, the new French food embodied an approach that would dramatically alter French cuisine. La Varenne, the chief cook to the socially and militarily prominent Marquis d'Uxelles, a Burgundian aristocrat and member of Louis xiv's Privy State Council, was primarily writing for members of his profession. Leaving the highly spiced foods of medieval Renaissance France behind, La Varenne's cooking emphasized the harmonious balance of the natural flavours of a particular dish rather than those of its individual components. No separate bits of parsley, chives or thyme found their way into his recipe for a meat bouillon. Instead there were bundles of herbs uniting those flavours that would be discarded after cooking.

Therefore, although recipes for compound salads existed, plain salad greens like lettuce, endive or rocket on their own were unlikely to get attention or approval. Instead, salad greens often became either garnishes or ingredients that, cooked and combined with other foods, created a new flavour. Lettuce, for example, turns up frequently in *Le Cuisinier françois*: as a garnish (sometimes cooked) for dishes such as chicken with green peas; as an ingredient in soups such as lettuce pottage with pea purée; or chopped with other raw vegetables and herbs to create a vegetable flavouring to be added to an omelette.

'Lettuce leaves are for garnishing all sorts of pottages', wrote La Varenne. 'Blanch them well, wash them and set to simmer in a pot with your best bouillon. On meat days, season them with anything fat; on lean days, add in some butter. As soon as they are cooked, split them in half and garnish your pottages with them.' That said, the lack of basic salad recipes in *Le Cuisinier françois* doesn't mean that they weren't served and eaten. Undoubtedly they were, but as usual, recipes weren't needed for greens and a dressing.

By 1740, according to the lawyer, politician, epicure and writer Jean-Anthelme Brillat-Savarin, in France a typical upper-class meal for ten would include salad in the second meat course. The dressing would surely have been a version

First page of *Le Cuisinier françois* (The French Cook) by François Pierre de la Varenne (first edition 1651).

LE
CVISINIER
FRANCOIS,
ENSEIGNANT LA MANIERE
de bien apprester, & assaisonner
toutes sortes de viandes, grasses
& maigres, legumes,
Patisseries, &c.

Reueu, corrigé, & augmenté d'vn
Traitté de Confitures seiches &
liquides, & autres delicatesses
de bouche.

Ensemble d'vne Table Alphabetique des
matieres qui sont traictées dans tout
le Liure.

Par le sieur de *LA VARENNE*, Escuyer de
Cuisine de Monsieur le Marquis d'Vxelles,
SECONDE EDITION,
A PARIS,
Chez PIERRE DAVID, au Palais, à l'entrée
de la Gallerie des Prisonniers.

M. DC. LII.
AVEC PRIVILEGE DV ROT.

of oil and vinegar. Brillat-Savarin recounts an amusing tale of one Monsieur Aubignac, an impecunious Frenchman living in London. One day while dining in a tavern there, young men eating in the same establishment noticed Aubignac, and asked him to mix a salad for them. After requesting the necessary ingredients, the displaced Frenchman proceeded to make the dressing. He was soon sought out to make salad dressing at fashionable homes all over London.

America

Despite the history of salads in Europe, the place where they would flourish and come into their own was America – and not only as a simple dish of greens and a dressing, or a heavily laden conglomeration, but as a main dish. Salads weren't written about much in the New World until after the Civil War. The disruptions to everyday life of the American Revolution and then the Civil War itself, with its decimation of agriculture in the South, could not have helped. Nevertheless, very basic, plain and undoubtedly local salads – a handful of greens, often put together from family gardens, a dressing – did exist. A few even appeared in cookbooks. Early salads were even a part of American tavern food, and commented on by foreign travellers. The writer François Rabelais noted that salads were served along with roast meats he saw in New York as far back as the late sixteenth century.

In the eighteenth century Brillat-Savarin, travelling in America, included salads among the foods he saw in New York eateries. 'Physically and morally armed,' he wrote, 'we went to the old bank coffee house, where we found our friends; dinner was soon ready. It consisted of a huge piece of beef, a roasted turkey, (plain) boiled vegetables, a salad and

An American invention, the Cobb salad with bacon, chicken breast and cheese.

pastry.' Although Brillat-Savarin didn't see fit to describe those salads, the plainness of the rest of the meal indicates that the vegetables were undoubtedly whatever was at hand, probably including some kind of raw leafy green, which would have provided a contrast to the boiled vegetables.

That said, the range of vegetables that could be used for salads was extensive. Christopher Sauer, an eighteenth-century German American apothecary and printer in Pennsylvania, considered 35 plants appropriate for salad, among them cabbage, endive, fennel, watercress, spinach, chard and radishes.

(Mysteriously, there is no mention of lettuce.) Herbs were plentiful, too: oregano, rosemary, saffron, summer savory, tarragon and thyme.

Sauer's book *Herbal Cures: America's First Book of Botanic Healing* echoed the much earlier food-as-medicine idea, and even employed Galenic terms to describe and recommend individual vegetables. Watercress, for example, was warm and dry, as was basil. 'Elderberry shoots eaten as a salad', Sauer wrote, 'will purge choler, water and phlegm with both emetic and laxative action'. Only a few decades later, however, as scientists began to realize that diseases had nothing to do with humours, this approach would become out of date. But to Sauer the healing properties of greens were very much alive,

Potato salad with parsley garnish.

Film star Esther Williams preparing a salad at the Del Mar Hotel, Los Angeles, 1947.

especially in a salad. 'The salad is an important dimension of curing', he wrote, 'because many herbs and greens completely lose their nutritional and medical properties when subjected to heat.'

Amelia Simmons, writing in 1796, didn't mention salads at all in her *American Cookery*. Discussing cabbages, she only mentioned slaw, perhaps indicating that if leafy greens and a dressing were desirable, no recipe was needed. Over time, as the country's culinary possibilities evolved, so did American salads. Not only did their content vary, but where, when and for what purposes they might be served. Salads could be assembled as a first course, a side-dish, a penultimate course or even in place of an entire meal. Recipes for salad found their way into American cookbooks in the mid-nineteenth century. By 1832, *The Cook's Own Book*, written by Boston housekeeper Mrs N.K.M. Lee, had a pretty straightforward description of simple green salads, and suggests dressing them in a way that is still recommended but not used often enough: by pouring the dressing down the sides of the salad bowl rather than over the salad itself. In 1838, in Mary Randolph's *The Virginia Housewife*, the compound salad tradition emerged (described there as 'salmagundi'). And in 1840 an early but recognizable recipe for chicken salad (chopped chicken and celery with a dressing of oil, vinegar, mashed hard-boiled egg yolks and English mustard) appeared in Eliza Leslie's *Directions for Cookery*. In 1883, the native of New York state Emma Pike Ewing devoted her *Cookery Manual No. 3* entirely to 'Salad and Salad Making', although by that time the definition of salad had expanded to include fruit salads, vegetable salads, fish salads, meat salads and mixed salads.

In the early twentieth century, the salad story became much more extensive. The simple greens-based salad continued to be popular and recipes abounded, while another salad development that would be endorsed by prominent cooking schools was in the works. Mary J. Lincoln, in her 1900 cookbook, embraced both the past and the future when she not only provided a salad of green vegetables cooked and served cold with a dressing, but then asserted that 'lobster, oysters, salmon, and other kinds of cooked fish, eggs, chicken, and delicate meats are combined with lettuce, cresses, or celery, and salad dressing.'

In 1907, in her *Best 250 Recipes*, the prolific cookbook author Sarah Tyson Rorer included an entire chapter on salad. The first recipe in that chapter is for a lettuce salad. What she described as her favourite was assembled with lettuce, cabbage, thin slices of boiled beetroot, celery seeds, salt and pepper, mint sauce, onion juice, soy or Worcestershire sauce, mushroom ketchup, garlic, olive oil and grape or tarragon vinegar. In 1912, she devoted an entire book to the subject: *New Salads for Dinners, Luncheons, Suppers and Receptions*. (She also wrote books on ice cream, leftovers, eggs, soups and sandwiches). Her guidance is still apt:

A dinner salad is composed of daintily cooked or raw green vegetables, dressed with French dressing about

Caesar salads are popular worldwide.

At the turn of the 20th century an extravagant salad might have included lobster meat.

4 or 5 parts oil to one of vinegar, with seasonings to harmonize . . . a suspicion of garlic or onion . . . with a drop or two of Worcestershire sauce.

Following what she saw as the French approach to salads, Rorer also offered guidance on when salads should be dressed (at the last moment) and the order in which the dressing ingredients should be added to the salad: first salt and pepper, then the oil from a spoon that has been rubbed with garlic, and finally, when the salad was mixed, the vinegar.

Fannie Farmer went even further, including both simple and compound salads in *The Boston Cooking-school Cook Book* of 1896. In a chapter on salads, she said that salads 'are now made in an endless variety of ways, and are composed of meat, fish, vegetables (alone or in combination) or fruits, with the addition of a dressing'. Soon enough, foods that really weren't traditional salads at all called themselves salads and made their way into cookbooks: fruit salads, party and dessert salads, moulded salads, vegetable salads, macaroni salads, rice salads, meat salads, poultry salads, seafood salads – and, later on in the century, the tuna, chicken, shrimp, egg and mayonnaise varieties.

The domestic science movement, which began in the late nineteenth century and was embraced by influential cooking schools in Boston, Philadelphia and New York, thought little of basic green salads. They were considered too haphazard – not organized, dainty or scientific enough for their taste. Salads that weren't organized into an orderly, pretty arrangement were found wanting. As Laura Shapiro explained in her illuminating *Perfection Salad* (1986), 'Salads that were nothing but a heap of raw ingredients in disarray plainly lacked cultivation.' Many of those recipes featured both green and non-green ingredients, but they were ladylike – not like the more hefty, traditional compound salads. They were more contained, more controlled, sometimes encased in lettuce cups, a red pepper ring or a tomato – even in gelatine.

That emphasis on composition and appearance was very much of its time. And by the mid-twentieth century, the wary attitude towards vegetables bequeathed by antiquity had finally disappeared, and salads were considered an everyday food, like soup or dessert.

Both plain and not-so-plain salads continued to be enjoyed. Some salads were simply mixed greens – hence the 'mixed salad' still seen on menus everywhere – or even just lettuce (occasionally garnished with grated carrots or tomato wedges), and were often served as side-dishes or appetizers. Others, such as a chef's salad, were more substantive main dishes, now thought of as 'main course' salads, rather than 'compound' or 'grand'. Still others were the kind that were conceived of and recommended as dietetic, like

Waldorf salad with walnuts, celery, apples, grapes and yoghurt.

the single-serving can of tuna plonked onto a plate of greens recommended by early WeightWatchers programmes.

In 1964, the *Favorite Recipes of Home Economics Teachers* considered greens the basis of all salads. 'The uses of salads are almost as varied as the kinds of salads from which to choose', the authors wrote.

> Most frequently, salads are served in medium-size portions as accompaniments to the meals, and are light rather than heavy . . . Small bits of tart fruit or seafood arranged on a bed of greens are appetite teasers and are often used as the first course of a meal . . . Hearty salads – those that contain meat, poultry or seafood with fresh raw or cooked vegetables – are a meal in themselves and are used as main dishes . . . Sweet salads are sometimes served as desserts and are used for special occasions.

That emphasis on composition and appearance was very much of its time. Inadvertently, that approach was a forerunner of

SALADS.

1.—Cucumber.   2.—Beetroot and Potato.   3.—Macédoine.   4.—Tomato.   5.—Russian.
6.—Italian.   7.—Prawn.   8.—Egg.   9.—Lobster.   10.—Salad Dumas.

Salad dish display from a 1907 edition of Mrs Beeton's *Book of Household Management*.

today's world, where – ideally – the visual and gastronomic play of individual ingredients with and against each other in chef-designed salads is carefully planned and thought out, where salads are so popular that new salad cookbooks sprout up regularly, and where cooking magazines proudly feature exquisitely designed new seasonal salads on a monthly basis.

4
New Countries Embrace Salads in the 20th and 21st Centuries

The Prior took me into the garden . . . Excellent salad, cabbages in perfection and such cauliflowers and artichokes as you will hardly find in Europe.

J. W. Goethe, from his late eighteenth-century drama
Goetz von Berlichingen

From the late nineteenth century on, and especially in the twentieth and twenty-first centuries, both plain and not-so-plain salads could be found on dinner tables throughout Western Europe and America. In parts of the world with less reliable springs and summers, hardier vegetables might also be embraced. And today, salads can be found on dinner tables all over the world – sometimes just as a handful of greens with oil and vinegar or lemon, at other times as an assemblage of raw or cooked and cooled vegetables bound with a more substantive dressing based on mayonnaise or even sour cream.

In less warm parts of Europe east or north of the Mediterranean, salads might feature leafy greens in summer but during the rest of the year rely on hardier vegetables, usually cooked and cooled. Many parts of Asia, South Asia and

Africa regularly face less hospitable climates and therefore have had less access to – or for that matter, interest in – raw leafy greens. In those places, salads often featured cooked vegetables, however they were prepared and served. Even so, salad-like dishes have emerged and continue to do so – sometimes with raw, sturdier vegetables, sometimes with cooked vegetables. The desire for contrast within a meal continues in many cuisines, and room-temperature vegetable dishes with a dressing have provided that. In some countries, ingredients that are an inherent part of the local cuisines (such as bean curd in China and seaweed in Japan) have been incorporated into dishes presented as salads. In addition, in today's global world, international visitors bring their eating habits with them when they travel, including a desire for salads. They may not be inherent parts of those food cultures, but they do exist, and some – especially on restaurant menus in hotels that serve an international clientele – even resemble Western salads, though not in the abundance in which they can be found in Western Europe and North America and not necessarily with the same primary ingredients.

Eastern and Northern Europe

Eastern European cuisines feature some of the same approach to salads found in Western Europe, especially in summer, when variations on lettuce salads with oil and vinegar dressings can be found throughout the region. Throughout the year, local vegetables such as radishes, beetroot, cucumbers, rhubarb, carrot, diced pickled gherkins and mushrooms, as well as dill, mustard seeds and red pepper, will be found in salads more frequently than they would be in Italy or France, as will cooked and then cooled vegetables rather than delicate

Beetroot cut into small slices or cubes can be found in salads in countries with a cold climate.

lettuces. In colder months, hardier vegetables or cooked vegetables might be used for salads.

In parts of Eastern Europe, Scandinavia and Russia, both raw and cooked-and-cooled vegetables are often used for salads. Cabbages, for example, might be cooked or raw, and the dressings for them are often made with sour cream rather than the olive oil produced in warmer climes. Germany, on the edge of Eastern Europe, is well known for its potato salads, generally made with an oil and vinegar combination, sometimes assisted by sliced onion and meat broth, but there are several regional variations. Sometimes cucumbers and dill enliven potato salads, and cucumber salad on its own is popular. Sausages can also be used for salads. Lamb's lettuce, when it is available, is prized in green salads. In Sweden and Denmark, many typically Scandinavian ingredients, including dressed cucumbers, potatoes, beetroot, apples and marinated herring, are used to construct salads. A particularly appealing one is a cucumber salad, which combines marinated thinly

Because the Bulgarian climate does not guarantee the availability of greens, hardier vegetables are often found in salads.

sliced cucumbers with salt, sugar and dill. Poland is not particularly well known for its salads, but when available, vegetables that are used in salads there include potatoes, radishes, beetroot, cucumbers, peas, rhubarb and carrots, as well as diced gherkins, mushrooms, dill, mustard seeds, red pepper and thyme. In Bulgaria, Shopska salad, a mid-twentieth-century invention, is enjoyed, particularly in summer. Made of tomatoes, cucumbers, peppers, sirene cheese (similar to feta), onion and parsley in a vinaigrette topped with a layer of grated or diced sirene cheese, Shopska salad is variously assembled throughout neighbouring parts of Europe, including Macedonia, Serbia, Bosnia and Croatia. Feta cheese might be substituted for sirene in areas where it is commonly available. There is also a Bulgarian green salad made with lettuce, radishes, cucumber, spring onions, white vinegar or lemon and oil.

Turkey

By virtue of its location bordering on the edge of Western Asia to the east, southeastern Europe to the west, and the Middle East to the south, as well as its maritime position straddling the Black and Mediterranean Seas, Turkey is home to many different food traditions. Salads are at home in Turkey – its green salads are usually accompanied by carrot shavings, cut-up tomatoes, sometimes cucumber slices and spring onions, as well as locally popular ingredients such as purslane, dandelion, spinach root and parsley. Lemon juice is often used instead of or alongside vinegar. But other salads are more specifically Turkish. One popular one is the shepherd's salad, which includes tomatoes, cucumbers, onions, parsley,

A Turkish speciality: kebab with salad.

sliced tomatoes, olive oil and lemon juice, and is frequently found in Turkish restaurants outside Turkey.

Other Turkish salads include a green lentil and bulgur salad, often made with tomatoes or tomato paste, spring onions, diced green peppers, tomatoes, chopped walnuts, parsley, lemon, dill and salt and pepper. Cooked vegetable salads (potatoes, carrots, peas, hard-boiled eggs, parsley, salt and pepper) might be dressed with white wine vinegar and olive oil rather than lemon.

Turkish salads on their own, as opposed to eaten as a side-dish or as a part of a selection of mezze, are often presented with chewy bread. However they are served, they provide an excellent contrast to a main dish of grilled or stewed meats or fish. A large number of other foods that are much heavier than green salads, but are still called salads, highlight sturdy ingredients such as cooked potatoes, white beans or aubergine (eggplant). White bean salad, for example, in addition to the cooked beans, is composed of parsley, tomatoes, onions, peppers, olive oil, lemon juice and occasionally hard-boiled eggs. A green lentil and bulgur salad, often served as a lunch dish, might also include chopped walnuts, spring onions, green pepper, tomato, basil, pepper, lemon, parsley and dill. In summer fresh fruit salad might also be served as an accompaniment to dinner.

Spain

Few countries have been home to as many diverse culinary influences as Spain – Roman, Arab, Islamic and Jewish cultures, each bringing its own eating habits, prohibitions, favoured crops and animals, and each making an impact on what today is thought of as Spanish food. Centuries later, vegetables brought back from the New World – among them corn, potatoes, tomatoes, pumpkins and avocados – became a part of Spanish cooking too, enriching the country's cuisine and arriving earlier there than in many parts of Europe.

Typical Spanish foods, as well as the dishes inherited and reconfigured from those traditions, however, are generally cooked. Salads depend on the land and the weather as much as on history, and of course on the goals of the salad makers. Today's Spain is the source of some of the most creative cooking in Europe and America and the salads there reflect both the country's heritage and its current status as a culinary star. Highlighting local ingredients, Anya von Bremzen's *The New Spanish Table* (2005) provides examples of both: a potato salad with sweet onion, a long, thin-skinned Italian frying pepper, tomato and extra virgin olive oil, with aged sherry vinegar; an Andalusian rice, prawn and broad bean salad; a frisée salad with pancetta, pears, honey, olive oil and red wine vinegar; a mesclun salad with figs, Cabrales cheese, honey, orange juice, shallots, olive oil and red wine vinegar. Among the salads in Claudia Roden's *The Food of Spain* (2011) are a dish composed of a variety of vegetables cooked until tender, and then dressed with olive oil, white wine vinegar or lemon juice with chopped parsley, tomato and hard-boiled egg; a salad of roasted red peppers and tomatoes with olive oil and finely chopped garlic; and two roasted vegetable salads – one of tomato with olives, eggs and tuna, and another of red peppers, small unpeeled red or white onions with olive oil, lemon juice, cumin and black olives. And in his *Tapas* (2005), chef José Andrés includes salads of frisée with blood oranges, goat's cheese, almonds and garlic; tomato, green peppers and cucumber with tuna; and Valencia oranges and pomegranates with an olive oil and sherry vinegar dressing.

Edible flowers add sophistication to salads.

Greens for salads are often grown near Russian dachas, like this one in the Izhevsk region of the Udmurt Republic.

Russia

The weather in Russia points salad lovers to vegetables that don't depend on long summers. Marinated beetroot, for example, can be presented as salad, as can julienned red cabbage in a marinade, or cucumbers with spring onions and dill or even a combination of carrots and apples. When aubergines are used for salads, they are often chopped with onion, parsley, garlic, lemon juice and olive oil. Even sauerkraut (drained) can be turned into a salad. When available, tomatoes and cucumbers are made into salads, sometimes with sour cream, and at other times with olive oil and vinegar. Lettuce, too, is sometimes served as a salad, with a sour cream dressing or with olive oil and vinegar, presumably an inheritance from French chefs working for the Russian aristocracy.

Asia

Western salads are not a part of Chinese cuisine – the season-ings, spices and cooking methods have nothing in common with the assertiveness of crisp raw vegetables and a dressing. 'The Chinese rarely eat raw vegetables and so have no trad-ition of eating salads', says Gloria Bley Miller in *The Thousand Recipe Chinese Cookbook* (1966). And when vegetables are served with a dressing – salad-style – they tend to be blanched rather than raw, a process that can emphasize the taste of the vegetable as much as if not more than the dressing. (Western-style oil and vinegar dressings have an assertive quality that can blur or mask the flavour of the vegetable.) The dressing used on blanched or cooked and cooled vegetables relies on various combinations of soy sauce, vinegar, salt and soy or sesame oils, and sometimes grated fresh ginger. There is even a Chinese version of mayonnaise, a dressing that can include eggs and ketchup and occasionally mustard. Those dressings might be applied to the vegetables and chilled a few minutes before serving, in contrast to the Western approach which ideally applies salad dressings at the very last minute.

In Japanese cuisine, many traditional ingredients are found in contemporary salads, such as seaweed, beansprouts, cucum-ber, cabbage, daikon radish, mizuna greens and sumaimo (a kind of sweet potato). Sesame oil and rice vinegar are frequently found in salad dressing, as are miso, soy sauce, mayonnaise, lemon (frequently for fish salads) and ginger (though not at the same time). Dressings are often assembled before use to let the flavours blend. Refreshing Japanese salads include seaweed and cucumber dressed with rice vinegar, sugar and salt; cellophane noodles and cucumber, dressed with soy sauce, rice vinegar, sesame oil, sugar and salt; daikon radish and wakame seaweed salad with mizuna greens and radish

Asian salads often feature local greens such as Japanese seaweed.

sprouts with a soy sauce, vinegar, sesame oil and sugar dressing;
shrimp and cucumber; seaweed and cucumber. Fish salads,
often accompanied by Asian vegetables and some kind of
Japanese noodle, are also popular, particularly with prawns.
Like all Japanese art forms, salads there are particularly beauti-
ful. An especially elegant tangy white salad is described in
Shizuo Tsuji's *Japanese Cooking: A Simple Art* (1980). Its ingredients include shiitake mushrooms cooked with dashi, soy
sauce and mirin, chicken breast fillets, marinated Japanese
cucumber, carrot slices, devil's tongue jelly, salt, sugar, soy
sauce and a white dressing of pressed tofu, sesame paste or
seeds, sugar, soy sauce, rice vinegar and mirin.

India

A huge country with different climates and geography, as well
as a variety of cultural, caste and class distinctions, India is
home to many different food traditions and tastes. British

rule there between 1848 and 1947 also left its mark on some eating patterns. Salad in India was a kind of extra for families who could afford to include non-essential foods, and was generally laid out on the table together with the other foods in a meal.

That said, room-temperature foods are an appealing contrast to cooked dishes throughout the country. The actress and food writer Madhur Jaffrey, who grew up in Delhi, remembers with pleasure eating raw vegetables such as grated carrot dressed with spices, mustard oil, herbs, salt and lemon juice, sometimes with green chillies, cut beans and coconut or mung beans. Beetroot or any vegetable that could be grated and chopped was also similarly prepared. 'There was always something like that on the table', she recalls. 'You'd wash your hands, and dive in, taking a morsel

Indian cucumber and peanut salad.

of food in your fingers. It provides contrast, spice, texture, and vitamins. It's delicious and tasty, and you get what you need in the first place.'

Salad traditions vary throughout India, and salad combinations – even similar ones – have different names, depending on the language spoken where they are served, and naturally the vegetables grown in that part of the country. Common salad ingredients include grated cucumber, carrots, green pepper, tomatoes, coconut, oil and vinegar or lime juice and mustard seed, and in South India also tamarind and plantains. Pickled vegetables might also be presented with meals as contrasts to cooked foods. Lentils are sometimes a part of salads, such as one made with carrots, cumin seeds, shredded coconut, coriander, lemon juice, ginger, sugar, salt and pepper. Even sliced raw onion can be presented as a salad when dressed with lemon juice, coriander and the spice mixture chaat masala. Seasonal fruit salads, sometimes made with yoghurt and rice, are also popular. Yoghurt, in fact, or more specifically raita, which is a variously seasoned version of yoghurt, is often used as a base – not a dressing – for a variety of foods, such as chopped or shredded vegetables, cooked pulses or fruit, which are then presented as a room-temperature dish as an accompaniment to hot foods. In South India, primary ingredients used for raita-based salads include okra, tomatoes, beetroot and tamarind. In some parts of South India, sago can also be used in salads.

Outside India and Pakistan, ingredients typically used in those cuisines are often used for salads in the West, resulting in dishes such as tandoori chicken salad, lentil salad, curried salad dressings and cumin- or tamarind-flavoured vinaigrettes.

Latin America

The extensive range of tropical fruits and vegetables grown in Latin America are the stars of their salads, adopted by both local chefs and home cooks. Jicama, mango, avocado, rocket, prickly pear, corn, coriander, hearts of palm and even cactus leaves are used in salads; so too are quinoa, beans or potatoes from Colombia, Argentina and Chile. Popular combinations include jicama with cucumber and lime, prickly pear with oranges and mint, watercress and hearts of palm with cherry tomatoes, Swiss chard with mustard greens and avocado with just about everything. Vinaigrettes for these salads often rely on tropical ingredients as well, like lime juice, pomegranate molasses and sometimes local honey.

Many South American countries have some versions of a criolla salad, served as a side-dish. In Argentina, its ingredients include lettuce, onions, tomato and often a chimichurri sauce. In Peru, the ingredients include red onion and yellow peppers. Beans and other legumes – red, white, black, green – play a role in many South American salads: chickpeas in Cuba, broad (fava) beans in Peru as part of *solterito*, a salad where the beans are accompanied by corn, sometimes potatoes and hot peppers. Beans, corns and peppers are also combined in some Mexican salads, as are avocados, jicama and cactus leaves, which, although available in cans, must be drained and rinsed in cold water before being used in salads. Mexican salad dressings are sometimes flavoured with lime rather than lemon or vinegar. Fruit salad is also popular in Mexico, where in some cities it is sold by street vendors, and often assembled in front of the customer. Ingredients vary depending on the season, and might include bananas, apples, strawberries, raisins, coconut or oranges, sometimes perked up with jicama or cucumber as

Chicken taco salad.

well as condensed milk, yoghurt or lime juice, the whole dusted with chilli powder.

A word about guacamole. Not technically a salad, guacamole uses similar ingredients, and provides a similar contrast to the main meal. Although there are several, almost subtle variants, Diana Kennedy's recipe in *The Art of Mexican Cooking* (1989) includes avocado, chopped white onion, chopped tomato and serrano chillies and is topped with more white onion, tomatoes and coriander.

Salads in Hawaii, the 49th state of the United States, have more in common with those in Latin America than in North America. By virtue of its climate and location, Hawaii is rich in local ingredients – fish, papayas, mangos or other tropical fruits – that play starring roles in salads. Hawaii's diverse culinary culture is also notable in its salad dressings, which might make use of soy sauce, Japanese vinegar, sesame oil, mirin or mayonnaise. Island fruit salads can feature tropical fruits, such as papayas, as well as fruits from more moderate climates, such as apples and pears.

5
Salad Dressings and Salad Siblings

The secret of a good salad is plenty of salt, generous oil, and a little vinegar.

Giacomo Castelvetro, 1614

Salads have been dressed with salt, oil and vinegar for hundreds of years – even as far back as Roman times. That tradition held on for centuries. Think back to Giacomo Castelvetro, that Italian exile in England who missed the fruits and herbs and vegetables of his homeland so much that he wrote a book about them. In what he called the Sacred Law of Salads, he was quite specific about how they should be dressed: 'Salt the salad quite a lot, then generous oil put in the pot, and vinegar, but just a jot.'

By then the salt, oil and vinegar approach had become predominant across Western Europe. In England, for example, at about the same time, a recipe for a salad of boiled vegetables in John Murrell's *A Newe Booke of Cookery* suggests a dressing of oil and vinegar or even butter and vinegar. About ten years later in Italy, the salad enthusiast Salvatore Massonio wrote: 'The ordinary seasoning of the salad is vinegar, oil and salt and . . . he who eats it without the dressing . . . loses the point of its name.' And in France around the same time,

Elegant glass cruets, French, 1763–4.

Rabelais' Gargantua enjoyed his green salad with a dressing of oil, vinegar and salt. That dressing would hang on for hundreds of years. It probably didn't taste exactly like the original versions, or even contemporary ones, but close enough.

Today, although a basic oil and vinegar is still the preferred dressing for many salad eaters, and is certainly not difficult to prepare, many consumers prefer more choices. The food industry has responded with olive oils from all over the world, with their own distinctive characteristics, and a continually growing multitude of bottled dressings with flavours ranging from blue cheese to creamy French to honey mustard and beyond that are available at just about any supermarket.

In that context, it's easy to forget the importance of just plain salt, which was the dressing used on the very earliest manifestations of salads. When the ingredients were bitter wild greens, salt must have made them palatable. Did that addition inspire experimentation that provided even more flavour? Probably, because by Galen's time, a fairly standard dressing usually comprised a salty preparation such as *garum* or another fermented fish sauce, an acid such as vinegar and olive oil. (Galen's entry on cabbage prescribes olive oil with fish sauce for cooked cabbage, but says that it doesn't make any difference if salt is used instead.) That said, by the late Middle Ages, that salty sauce had given way to the salt, vinegar and oil approach that became the default dressing for hundreds of years. It probably didn't taste precisely like contemporary vinaigrettes, but close enough.

Over time, other dressings emerged, and by the nineteenth century recipes for a variety of dressings found their way into cookbooks designed for home use. By 1884 in America, salads and their dressings had evolved enough to prompt Emma Pike Ewing, in her *Salad and Salad Making*,

Picking greens for a salad for Sunday dinner in 1942, Escambia Farms, Florida.

to describe four different kinds of dressings appropriate to different kinds of salads: transparent dressings (generally sweet or acidic for use on fruit salads, which had become popular but not at all interchangeable with green salads), French dressings (oil, vinegar, salt and pepper, and sometimes mustard), cream dressings (cream, cooked with flour, butter and flavourings, either sweet or savoury; sour cream, hot cream), and mayonnaise-based dressings. She cautioned against too heavy a hand. 'A dressing, whether of salt, sugar, vinegar, or a combination of many things should not be the prominent of main feature of a salad', she wrote. 'It should be only a dressing – an adjunct, to tone down and soften

Creamy dressings are a traditional way of dressing salads.

too sharp an acid, or too pungent a flavor, or to render finer or more distinctive some peculiar individuality of the fruits, vegetables, etc. composing the salad. This is the true mission of the dressing.'

Nevertheless, the oil, vinegar and salt approach carried on. 'Three parts of olive oil to one part of vinegar, with a pinch of salt and pepper is the foundation of French dressing – the standard dressing', wrote Henry Kegler in the 1921 *Fancy Salads of the Big Hotels*. 'All other dressings are made by mixing other ingredients with French dressing, such as mustard, spices, herbs, paprika, etc.'

At around the same time, a new American ingredient – commercial mayonnaise – appeared and transformed the approach to salad dressings. Richard Hellmann, a delicatessen owner in New York, was one of the first to see its possibilities. In 1912 Hellmann started selling his mayonnaise on a small scale from his delicatessen in Manhattan – first in one-gallon stone jars, then in smaller ones, and then, as the demand for the product grew, in bottles, which he had adorned with a label depicting three blue ribbons. The demand for his product was so great that he closed the delicatessen and moved the mayonnaise operation to facilities first in downtown Manhattan and then in Long Island City. Distribution and plants that made commercial mayonnaise outside Manhattan followed, including factories in Chicago (in 1919) and San Francisco (in 1922). Other manufacturers, small and large, jumped in. Consumers liked the spoonable dressing. They also liked the pourable dressings that the Kraft company introduced, starting with French dressing in 1925 and Kraft Miracle Whip in 1933.

Many earlier salads had incorporated home-made mayonnaise, but commercial mayonnaise made things much easier, and American cookbooks of the time reflect that. In the 1931

Hellmann's advertisement for mayonnaise.

edition of Irma S. Rombauer's *Joy of Cooking*, for example, the recipes in the salad section start out with lettuce and more or less standard salads made with greens and other vegetables, but quickly move along to include the newer salads such as potato salad with mayonnaise; cucumber and pineapple salad held together with either mayonnaise or French dressing; melon and cottage cheese with optional mayonnaise; and cucumber and pineapple salad with either mayonnaise or French dressing.

With the development of commercial mayonnaise, salads were no longer either simple or compound. The newcomers were made of a single ingredient plus mayonnaise, thereby creating a kind of salad sibling. Salads made with chicken and a type of vinaigrette had existed in nineteenth-century America, but commercial mayonnaise expanded and transformed the possibilities. The results were dishes known as salads but without salad greens. Instead, they were proteins (hard-boiled eggs, shrimp or the pride of them all: canned tuna), or a starch (potato, macaroni), or vegetable (string

Hellmann's
mayonnaise,
sold since 1912.

beans, cucumber) and mayonnaise. Often a bit of chopped celery – a hangover from nineteenth-century chicken salads – was introduced into the mix, giving the salad a needed fresh crunch. None of these salads was a traditional salad – either simple or compound. But it no longer mattered. The signifier of this new form of salad was the dressing.

Soon enough, commercial dressings with a mayonnaise base expanded to include flavourful (and sweeter) dressings such as Russian and Thousand Island (with pickle relish and ketchup); Green Goddess (with sour cream, chives, tarragon, lemon juice and sometimes chervil and anchovies); and Ranch (with buttermilk, salt, garlic, herbs like chives, parsley and dill, and sometimes cream or yoghurt). So, too, exotic versions

Advertising card for Bugbee & Brownell's salad dressing, 1870–1900.

Herbs, anchovies and sour cream turn mayonnaise into Green Goddess dressing.

of oil-and-vinegar-based dressings in an extensive variety of styles and flavours – chilli powder, honey mustard, rice wine and sesame, vegan and soy, to name a few – continue to be developed, and are eagerly purchased.

Some families favour these bottled dressings and bypass oil and vinegar altogether. Although many home cooks and restaurant chefs generally prefer to at least start with that more traditional approach, they may be a dwindling breed. The straightforward dressing that began with salt, oil and vinegar has morphed into aisles full of store-bought brands that are sweeter, saltier and more loaded with calories.

Today salad dressings show no signs of restraint. Urging home cooks to 'give weeknight salads a makeover', the Food

Network offers up fifty different salad dressings, including more-or-less standards such as classic vinaigrette, bistro bacon, Mediterranean, Dijon and creamy Italian as well as shockers like maple walnut, chocolate-balsamic and red raspberry. The very popular *Cooking Light Magazine* also provides a classic vinaigrette recipe, as well as four-herb Green Goddess, chilli-garlic, cranberry vinaigrette, creamy Caesar, blue cheese, herbed lemon buttermilk, ginger sesame, walnut oil, orange-fennel, cilantro (coriander) chilli, and grapefruit poppy seed dressings.

And that's just for starters.

6

From Lettuce Leaves to Farmers' Markets and Foam

> How do you make a salad? There's no rocket science involved.
> Just get your hands on some crisp, fresh greens; add a few other
> well-chosen ingredients; and toss with a flavor-packed dressing.
> That's the ball game.
>
> Chris Schlesinger and John Willoughby, *Lettuce in Your Kitchen*

Salads have travelled a long way since privileged eaters in antiquity dipped lettuce leaves in fermented fish sauce. Over time, salads have gone mainstream and today are so popular that a wide selection of salads appear on just about every restaurant and cafeteria menu and are featured in most standard cookbooks. The centuries-old wary view of raw vegetables has long been replaced by an enthusiastic appreciation for their vitamins, antioxidants and fibre. Salad eating is considered virtuous, as in 'I'll just have a salad' – an alternative to only theoretically more calorie-laden sandwiches or full meals. Takeout chains specialize in salads with a multitude of ingredients (vegetal and not) and dressings.

At the same time, a growing interest in vegetarianism and vegan eating has encouraged the growth of salad bars and restaurant salad menus – and not only in the United States and Britain. In many European cities – Paris, Rome, Berlin,

Vegetables, salad and fruits at a market in Majorca, Spain.

Copenhagen, Vienna, even Gdansk – it is no longer unusual to find restaurants with telling names like Green is Better (Paris), Saladette and Freunde (Berlin) and the Sweet Leaf Community Café (Vienna). In Asian and African cuisines salads are a more modern idea, but there too the Western concept of salad has emerged – often rethought in the light of specific local culinary habits, or sometimes adapted from the West. Menus from kitchens with an inevitably international clientele, such as those at hotel restaurants, often include Western salads. And chefs all over the world consider salads a tempting platform for creativity.

That said, wherever salads are served, greens – usually fresh but sometimes cooked and cooled – and a flavourful dressing are still the jumping-off point. With the growth of farmers' markets – in 2014 an estimated 550 in the UK and 8,268 in the United States (up from 1,755 in 1994) – and the increasing availability of salad ingredients way beyond industrially grown lettuce and tomatoes that fit in packing boxes, making a good salad is easier than ever. Some ingredients – tomatoes, onions, spinach, watercress, parsley, mint, spring onions, chives and carrots – have been commonly available in the u.s. and uk for decades. But many others – sweet peppers, avocados, rocket, endive, many kinds of sprouts and cresses, fennel, chard and even edible flowers in season, and of course fresh thyme, tarragon, basil and oregano – are now easy to obtain. It's no longer surprising to see what were once thought to be exotic vegetables, such as baby artichokes and rocket, on grocery shelves, and Asian and African greens are available at many speciality markets.

For people pressed for time, or who simply don't feel like preparing the ingredients, the popular plastic bags of ready-to-eat greens in the United States, the uk, throughout Europe and even in Japan have made a variety of salads easy to construct. Available in varying styles – among them American, Italian blend, spring mix, baby greens, mache, romaine, radicchio, rocket, slaw-style shredded vegetables and Asian

Édouard Vuillard, *Still-life with Salad Greens*, c. 1887–8.

A contemporary salad with bulgur wheat and parsley.

greens – these products allow consumers to assemble salads of their choice, even with out-of-season greens. (That picture, though convenient, is not entirely rosy: often industrially produced, in recent years, bagged and washed greens have been the cause of occasional outbreaks of foodborne illness such as listeria and salmonella, sometimes requiring national recalls.)

Jarred and bottled salad dressings, including organic, low-fat and flavoured varieties, are as numerous, various and specialized as wines, while an increasing variety of olive oils and vinegars are available – even in supermarkets. And different kinds of lettuces – from the beginning, the stalwart base of salads – are industrially grown not only in predictable places like the United States, Italy and France but in Japan, China, Thailand and India.

Although salads tend to be offered as a first course in restaurants, they are often a main, last or penultimate course in homes. Popular food magazines increasingly provide feature articles that highlight salads with a variety of ingredients including meats and cheeses as complete meals. And the accoutrements of salads – salad bowls, salad servers, salad spinners, salad forks, salad plates – are available at every price point and are popular wedding gifts. Nowadays, there are even professional associations that support salads: in Great Britain, the British Leafy Salad Association, in the United States, the Association for Dressings and Sauces, a group that represents international manufacturers of salad dressing, as well as dips, mustard, mayonnaise and salsas.

Crudités – technically not salads, but certainly first cousins to them – are popular too. Although these composed plates of cut and trimmed raw vegetables, often topped or served

The salad bowl: advertisement for mayonnaise.

with an oil and vinegar dressing, are not necessarily green, not mixed together and not served with a salad fork, they often replace salads as a first course, particularly in France or in French restaurants. And platters of them are a welcome sight in private homes and at catered meals. (There is no known history of the preparation of crudités, but just as for plain green salads, there is no reason to assume that chefs or home cooks needed an actual recipe for a plate of cut and trimmed raw vegetables accompanied by a dressing.)

Much of the longevity of salads can be traced to a twentieth-century development that would startle the ancients: salads are considered healthful foods. Eaten wisely, salads are an excellent inclusion in a balanced diet. A 2006 study on salad and raw vegetable consumption and their nutritional effect on thousands of adults conducted by the Louisiana State University School of Public Health concluded that salad consumers tended to have considerable amounts of vitamins C and E and other nutrients in their blood, and that eating salads

Mixed vegetables in small glasses.

Chicken livers add iron to green salads.

could not only help people exceed the u.s. recommended dietary allowance for vitamin C but could be an effective strategy for increased nutrition in the public at large.

Salads are also essential to that particularly twentieth- and twenty-first century obsession: dieting. Ever since a fashion for slim figures took hold, those with less than perfect bodies have tried to restrict their diets, and as a result were often hungry. Salads, because of their bulk, generally help appease hunger. When salads are served at the beginning of a meal, as is often the case at weight-reduction spas, they can contribute to a feeling of fullness desired by dieters. Salads served at the end of the meal offer the dieter the pleasure of an extra course, or serve as dessert. Salads also provide a light, nutritious and fresh-tasting component of lower-calorie meals – that is, as long as they aren't drenched in dressing and loaded with high-calorie add-ons such as cheese, bacon and croutons. (In restaurants, one way to avoid that near-inevitability is the late twentieth-century and now common

A dietician prepares salads for the noon meal at Schaumberg High School in Palatine, Illinois, February 1986.

request for 'dressing on the side': an instruction to waitstaff that lets diners avoid salads drenched with fat- or sugar-laden dressings.)

The healthful identity of salads without heavy dressings, their fresh taste and the proliferation of possible ingredients have inspired chefs and cookbook authors to come up with salad books of every conceivable variety. Recipes in this burgeoning cookbook category go far beyond the few leaves of lettuce and slices of tomato that in the mid-twentieth century used to satisfy the basic demands of a side salad. Some stress nutrition, others creativity, flavour or aesthetics. There are books for everyday salads, side salads, main-dish salads, different salads for every day of the year, authentic salads, rapid weight-loss salads, gluten-free salads, salads for WeightWatchers or Atkins dieters. There are books of so-called salad diets, which recognize the bulk that salad vegetables can provide as appealing to calorie counters; of salad dressings; and even of salads that specifically don't contain lettuce.

The consumer's appetite for salads led to the creation of the wildly successful 'salad bar' within restaurants, cafeterias and even fast-food outlets. Although particularly popular in the United States and the UK, salad bars are now also prized as far afield as Gibraltar, Budapest, Krakow, Moscow and even Beijing. Generally a long table with containers of ingredients that can go into a salad – from greens, to sliced or chopped vegetables, to more substantial add-ins such as canned tuna, cubed cooked chicken and chickpeas – salad bars have also become staples of moderately priced restaurants.

In recent years, the salad bar idea has become a mainstay of upmarket take-away places and even the star of franchises

Salad bar with a variety of options.

Chop't, a New York-based salad chain with branches in other cities.

almost exclusively devoted to salads that are primarily directed toward the urban lunch crowd. Just Salads is a chain with locations in New York City, Hong Kong and Singapore that offers a variety of salads, wraps, soups, frozen yoghurt and smoothies. Tossed is a franchise operation with locations in major American cities such as Boston, Houston and Los Angeles that offers made-to-order salads and wraps that proclaim 'Fifty fresh ingredients and home-made dressings'. Chop't, an upscale take-out chain where salads are the main attraction, boasts multiple branches in New York City and Washington, DC, and is still growing. Its long queues are an indication of the increasing attraction salads have for the consumer market – particularly the urban professional market. Founded by New Yorkers Tony Shure and Colin McCabe when they were in college, Chop't grew out of their desire for healthful delicious food, which was then rarely found on many university campuses. Aided by a how-to-write-a-business-plan book, they came up with salad take-out places based on fresh food delivered in a sleek urban setting, complete with seasonal additions to their menu, online ordering and delivery and a frequent-user loyalty programme.

Once home cooks, restaurant kitchens and the salad bar crowd discovered that there were no fixed rules for what went into salads, the historic line between simple and composed salads became blurred. Even though fairly straightforward mixed salads and green salads still have their place on many menus, salads have become a way that both chefs and home cooks can demonstrate their personal palates and flights of fancy. They have also become a platform for many different proteins, both hot and cold. And for those with a taste for molecular gastronomy, up-to-the-minute salads can be deconstructed and reassembled not only with dressings but with commercial, restaurant or even home-made vegetable foams. That 'no rules' approach has also encouraged a relaxed attitude to when salads are served: although they tend to be offered as a first course in restaurants, they are often a main, last or penultimate course in homes.

These days the future looks good for salads. They have become a popular – even predictable – part of meals eaten at home. And it's almost impossible to construct a restaurant menu without a variety of salad options. Who would have thought that what started out many centuries ago as an occasional extra – that plate of greens designed to be dipped in a salty sauce – would become a worldwide staple, and an essential food category that embodies a culture that emphasizes health and a preference for fresh and local ingredients.

Appendix:
Celebrity Salads

Caesar Salad
A reliable old salad that is all too often marred by bottled dressing, the Caesar salad has romanticized origins that even include Wallis Warfield Simpson as an early aficionado. The original 'recipe' is said to have been improvised by Tijuana restaurateur Caesar Cardini late one night in 1924 when he looked in the restaurant's larder and found romaine lettuce, garlic, croutons, Worcestershire sauce, Parmesan cheese and anchovies. Despite its age, the salad continues to be a popular selection on hotel, restaurant and even coffee-shop menus all over the world. Diners are often given the option to embellish the salad with a protein such as chicken, prawns or salmon, and, for that matter, to order it without anchovies. The dressing is a key feature of a Caesar salad. A u.s. patent for 'Cardini's Original Caesar dressing mix' was awarded in 1948, but countless salad-dressing companies offer their own bottled versions.

Chef's Salad
A bowl filled with greens topped by individual mounds of julienned ham, chicken or turkey, Swiss cheese, sometimes an egg and slices of avocado, the chef's salad enjoyed great popularity in the United States in the 1940s, '50s and '60s. A twentieth-century heir to the salmagundi salad of the seventeenth century and the even older compound or 'grand sallet', the chef's salad has fallen out of favour in recent years. Perhaps, like the Cobb salad, the

chef's salad is less popular than it was in the 1960s because of its enormous calorie count and considerable amount of fat. Ironically, the same contents and even many more, with attendant fat and calories, can be put together at most contemporary salad bars.

Several chefs' names are invoked in the history of the Chef's salad: Victor Seydoux at the Hotel Buffalo in Buffalo, New York, Jacques Roser at the Hotel Pennsylvania in Manhattan, and Louis Diat, chef at the Ritz-Carlton in New York in the 1940s, who was able to introduce the salad to a wide audience. The salad became so popular that some restaurants put together their own versions with minimal changes, like the chopped chives added by the Beverly Hills Brown Derby outpost, which called its rendition the Beverly Salad Bowl.

Chinese Chicken Salad

Certainly not Chinese, this dish of shredded or cubed cooked chicken breast, cabbage, carrots, canned water chestnuts and a dressing based on soy sauce, toasted sesame oil and often rice vinegar seems to have originated in Los Angeles. Recipes for it that aimed for heightened flavour and crunch exist from the late 1930s on and have included ingredients such as chilli sauce, ginger, garlic, chow mein noodles, canned mandarin oranges, walnuts, peanut butter, lime juice and red bell peppers. A popular luncheon dish, it has become ubiquitous throughout the United States.

Cobb Salad

Richer than the Caesar salad, the Cobb salad assembled an almost irresistible combination of lettuce (iceberg, but now also romaine), cubes of avocado, bacon, chicken breast or ham, blue cheese, sometimes tomato and a vinaigrette dressing.

Although the salad was named for Robert H. (Bob) Cobb, the owner of the Hollywood Brown Derby restaurant in Los Angeles, there are varying explanations of just when that occurred. Although some sources point to 1929, *The Brown Derby Restaurant*, a book written by Bob Cobb's widow Sally Wright Cobb and Mark Willems, dates the salad to 1937 when, the story goes, Cobb put it together late one night with refrigerator leftovers and some bacon. The recipe preserved in the book also includes watercress, chicory, chopped chives, hard-boiled eggs, grated Roquefort cheese and the restaurant's old-fashioned French dressing. The salad was served with the restaurant's pumpernickel cheese toast: paper-thin slices of buttered pumpernickel bread sprinkled with Parmesan cheese and toasted under a hot grill (broiler).

The classic Cobb, which was and is delicious but undoubtedly high in calories and fat, is still served, but contemporary chefs often offer it in a trimmed-down, more modern version.

Coleslaw

A descendant of the Dutch *koolsla* or *koolsalade* (cabbage salad in Dutch), coleslaw is essentially a finely shredded cabbage salad dressed with mayonnaise, buttermilk or a vinaigrette. Coleslaw has a long history. Dressings and additions vary, and tend to be regional, some emphasizing a creamy dressing, some employing a more vinegary approach. Although the basic ingredient in classic coleslaw is pale green cabbage, red cabbage may be substituted. Common flavourings include celery seeds and vinegar. Coleslaw is generally served as a side-dish with sandwiches, hamburgers, barbecue or fried chicken, but can also be an ingredient in layered sandwiches, particularly pastrami and corned beef. Bagged pre-sliced slaw vegetables (cabbage, broccoli and root vegetables) can be found in many supermarkets. Coleslaw is probably the most ubiquitous salad in the United States.

Cottage Cheese and Fruit

Not technically a salad, this classic diet dish is usually listed as one on menus, though that classification depends entirely on the amount and kind of cottage cheese as well as the amount and kind of fruit on the plate. It is immensely enlivened by a judicious splash of balsamic vinegar. It is generally preferred (or thought to be) by women.

Greek Salad

Probably made without lettuce in its original configuration, today the world over the Greek salad is a chunky dish made of pieces of tomatoes, cucumber, feta cheese, olives and oregano (both ideally Greek), oil and vinegar. Variations exist, usually a result of the availability of the traditional ingredients. Cypriot salads, for example, are similar, varying only with local ingredients and sometimes the addition of finely sliced cabbage and/or lettuce. Like the Salade Niçoise, the Cobb and the Caesar salad, the Greek salad is a familiar item on menus in American diners, which traditionally have been owned and run by Greeks.

Insalata Caprese
A Neopolitan dish, the Insalata Caprese alternates slices of top-quality ripe tomatoes and fresh mozzarella cheese, dressed with olive oil, salt and fresh basil. It is served as a starter, as part of antipasti, or even as a main dish for lunch.

Israeli Salad
Some scholars insist that this salad of finely chopped tomatoes, cucumbers, onions and parley with a dressing of lemon juice, olive oil and sometimes garlic or mint is really an Arab salad. No matter – the dish is served throughout the eastern Mediterranean and Arab world and in restaurants featuring that cuisine. Although offered on restaurant menus on its own, it is often served as part of a buffet or as an accompaniment to blander foods.

Larb
Larb is a spicy salad from Northern Thailand and Laos of minced chicken (or pork or beef) and toasted ground rice served at room temperature with lettuce leaves. Lettuce-leaf-wrapped bundles of the salad are dipped in a dressing of fish sauce, grated lime zest or kaffir lime leaves, sometimes honey, shallots, dried chilli pepper or one small Thai chilli, fresh mint and coriander (cilantro). The bundles are served at room temperature, usually as a first course.

Lettuce and Tomato Salad
From the late nineteenth century through to the 1950s, the basic lettuce and tomato salad was perhaps the most common American salad. It could be dressed up with a mayonnaise garnish,

as Fannie Farmer suggested in the *Boston Cooking School Cook Book* of 1896. It could be put together with little fanfare as a first course or a side-dish in both modest restaurants and family dining rooms. And, until tomatoes were subjected to industrial farming, the salad probably tasted pretty good. Now, after the renewed popularity of farmers' markets in the late twentieth century, a variety of fresh lettuces and tomatoes can be assembled without shame.

Panzanella

This Tuscan summer salad made of stale bread (originally the bread left over from the week's baking), ripe tomatoes, basil, good olive oil and usually vinegar is impossible to date. Early pre-tomato versions of a bread salad were known to exist in Italy. But the arrival of tomatoes from the New World transformed the salad. Today, chefs are even fussier and want only fine, ripe tomatoes. Recipes used to demand first soaking the bread in water, and then squeezing the water out, but these days many recipes skip that step and moisten the bread by combining all the ingredients at the same time. Although not traditional, contemporary recipes occasionally employ red onion, garlic and even celery or cucumbers in the mix. It has been noticed that the colours of the salad (red, white and green) echo those of the Italian flag.

Salade Lyonnaise

A traditional French dish, the salade Lyonnaise is said to have been enjoyed by the silk workers of Lyon in the seventeenth and eighteenth centuries. The salad combines greens (usually frisée), warm bacon chunks, a soft-boiled egg, occasionally anchovies and an oil and vinegar dressing. Often presented as a starter, the salad is ample enough to be served as the main dish it originally was. In the United States, the popularity of this delicious and satisfying salad may be related to its familiar combination of bacon and egg.

Salade Niçoise

An international favourite, the salade Niçoise pays homage to the city of Nice in the South of France. Its origins are unclear – some histories even point back to the cooks brought by Catherine de' Medici when she came to France in 1533 to marry the future king Henri II. That said, the popular twentieth- and twenty-first-century version, often served on a plate rather than in a bowl, is assembled with cooked green beans, canned (ideally oil-packed) tuna, hard-boiled eggs, tomatoes, olives, sometimes anchovies and a vinaigrette dressing. Contemporary restaurant versions usually substitute cooked fresh tuna for canned, but aficionados generally prefer canned. Niçoise is one of the most popular main-dish salads in the world.

Tabbouleh
A salad from the Levantine Arab world, especially the mountains of Syria and Lebanon, tabbouleh is traditionally made of bulgur wheat, finely chopped parsley, tomatoes, cucumbers, mint, onions, olive oil and lemon juice. An easy to prepare dish, tabbouleh is generally served as part of a mezze, and has become popular internationally.

Waldorf Salad
The Waldorf salad, a combination of chopped apples, celery, mayonnaise and eventually chopped walnuts on a bed of lettuce, is a turn-of-the-century creation. Its recipe is generally credited to Oscar Tschirky, the dapper maître d'hotel who once served it at a dinner for 1,500 guests and included it in his book, *The Cookbook by Oscar of the Waldorf* (1896). The Waldorf salad clearly had staying power – Cole Porter mentioned it approvingly in the lyrics of 'You're the Top', one of the songs in the 1934 musical *Anything Goes*: 'You're the top, you're a Waldorf salad. You're the top, you're a Berlin ballad.' In the twenty-first century, the Waldorf salad might be served as a side-dish, as one among other salads, or on its own.

Wedge Salad
A chunk (or wedge) of iceberg lettuce topped with abundant blue cheese dressing, this salad is often found in American steakhouses. Heavy with calories in its basic form, it can be even more calorific

when topped with crumbled blue cheese, bacon bits or chopped tomato. The Wedge is a sentimental American favourite, even of sophisticated diners.

Recipes

Although the recipes in this book specify sizes and amounts of ingredients, salads by their very nature involve an inevitable degree of flexibility. One head of romaine lettuce is rarely the same size as another. Some lemons are more tart than others. Summer tomatoes are more flavourful than greenhouse varieties. Even basic vinegars and oils are variable in taste and texture. Cooks are encouraged to adapt these recipes according to their own preferences.

Historic Recipes

Mixed Salad
Platina, *c.* 1473–5

A mixed salad is prepared with lettuce, oxtongue, mint, catnip, fennel, parsley, watercress, oregano, chervil, chicory and dandelion greens (described by doctors as taraxacum and arnoclossa), wonderberry, fennel flowers and various other aromatic herbs, well washed and drained. These are placed in a large dish and flavoured with abundant salt. Oil is added, and vinegar sprinkled on top. The salad is then left to macerate for a short while. Because of the coarseness of the ingredients, one must be careful to chew thoroughly when eating.

Excellent Mixed Salads
Giacomo Castelvetro, late sixteenth century

Of all the salads we eat in the spring, the mixed Salads, which I am about to describe, are the best known and loved of them all. This is how we make them: take young leaves of mint, those of nasturtium, basil, salad burnet, tarragon, the flowers and tenderest leaves of borage, the flowers of herba stella [buck's horn plantain], the newborn shoots of fennel, the leaves of rocket, of sorrel, or lemon balm, rosemary flowers, some sweet violets, and the tenderest leaves of the hearts of lettuce. When these precious potherbs have been picked clean and washed in several waters, and dried a little with a clean linen cloth, they are dressed, as usual, with oil, salt and vinegar.

Poetic Salad
Sydney Smith, early nineteenth century

The Reverend Sydney Smith lived from 1771 to 1845. There are two versions of this poetic recipe; this one was recorded by John Timbs, a nineteenth-century English author and antiquary.

Two large potatoes, passed through kitchen sieve
Unwonted softness to the salad give
Of mordent mustard add a single spoon
Distrust the condiment which bites so soon.
But deem it not, thou man of verbs, a fault,
To add a double quantity of salt;
Three times the spoon with oil of Lucca crown,
And once with vinegar, procured from town.
True flavour needs it, and your poet begs
The Pounded yellow of two well-boiled eggs.
Let onion atoms lurk within the bowl,
And scarce suspected animate the whole,
And lastly, on the flowery compound toss

A magic soupspoon of Anchovy sauce.
Then though green turtle fail, though venison's tough,
And ham and turkey are not boiled enough,
Serenely full, the Epicure may say –
Fate cannot harm me, I have dined today.

To Make Salamongundy

Hannah Glasse, *The Art of Cookery* (1747)

Take two or three Roman or Cabbage Lettice, and when you have washed them clean, swing them pretty dry in a Cloth; then beginning at the open End, cut them cross-ways, as fine as a good big Thread, and lay the Lettices so cut, about an Inch thick all over the Bottom of the Dish. When you have thus garnished your Dish, take a Couple of cold roasted Pullets, or Chickens, and cut the Flesh off the Breasts and Wings into Slices, about three Inches long, a Quarter of an Inch broad, and as thin as a Shilling; lay them upon the Lettice round the End to the Middle of the Dish and the other towards the Brim; then having boned and cut six Anchovies each into eight Pieces, lay them all between each Slice of the Fowls, then cut the lean Meat of the Legs into Dice, and cut a Lemon into small Dice; then mince the Yolks of four Eggs, three or four Anchovies, and a little Parsley, and make a round Heap of these in your Dish, piling it up in the Form of a Sugar-loaf, and garnish it with Onions, as big as the Yolk of Eggs, boiled in a good deal of Water very tender and white. Put the largest of the Onions in the Middle on the Top of the Salamongundy, and lay the rest all round the Brim of the Dish, as thick as you can lay them; then beat some Sallat-Oil up with Vinegar, Salt and Pepper and pour over it all. Garnish with Grapes just scalded, or French beans blanched, or Station [nasturtium] Flowers, and serve it up for a first Course.

Modern Recipes

Basic Vinaigrette Dressing

1 cup (225 ml) olive oil
¼–⅓ cup (55–75 ml) vinegar
salt and pepper to taste
2 tsp Dijon mustard, if desired

Combine the salt, pepper, mustard (if using) and vinegar in a small bowl and mix well. Slowly add the olive oil while stirring until blended.

Chef's Salad

Food historians disagree about the origin of the chef's salad, attributing it to various chefs at prominent hotels in both New York or California in the 1940s. It is usually presented as a main dish.

6–8 cups (300–400 g) washed and dried salad greens, including red leaf lettuce, or a mixture
4 oz (100 g) Swiss cheese, cut into thin strips
4 oz (100 g) baked ham, cut into thin strips
4 oz (100 g) cooked chicken, or turkey breast
2 shelled, peeled and sliced hard-boiled eggs
1 ripe avocado, diced into ½-inch (3-cm) pieces
1 cup cherry tomatoes, halved
1 cup vinaigrette (see recipe above)

Put salad greens in a large bowl. Add the remaining ingredients and toss. Just before serving, slowly add the vinaigrette, being careful not to overdress the salad.
Serves 4 to 6

Cobb Salad

A classic American salad created in 1937 at The Brown Derby in Los Angeles by the restaurant's owner, Robert Cobb. It is usually presented as a main dish.

For the salad:
1 head iceberg or romaine lettuce, washed, dried and chopped into 1- to 2-inch (3–5 cm) strips
½ bunch watercress, roughly chopped
1 boneless, skinless, cooked chicken breast, cut into bite-size pieces
2 oz (50 g) blue cheese, crumbled
1 ripe avocado, cut into ½- to 1-inch (1–2 cm) pieces
3 to 4 medium tomatoes, peeled, seeded and cut into 1-inch (3-cm) pieces
6 strips cooked bacon, crumbled

For the dressing:
4 tbsp good quality olive oil (rapeseed/canola oil may be substituted)
1 tbsp good quality vinegar
2–3 tsp lemon juice
1 tsp Dijon mustard
salt and pepper to taste

Combine the dressing ingredients in a small bowl. Stir well. In a large bowl combine the lettuce and watercress and arrange on a large platter. Place the chicken breast, blue cheese, bacon, tomatoes and avocado in neat rows atop the salad greens. Drizzle the dressing all over the salad.

Serves 4 as a main dish

Waldorf Salad

For the salad:
1 head Boston or Romaine lettuce
3 small to medium-size tart apples, cleaned, peeled, cored and diced
2–3 cleaned celery stalks, cut into ½-inch (1-cm) pieces, yielding about same amount as the apples
½ to ¾ cup (50–60 g) toasted chopped walnuts
¼ cup (40 g) raisins

For the dressing:
½ to ⅔ cup (110–150 ml) good mayonnaise, preferably home-made
lemon juice to taste
salt and pepper to taste

To prepare the dressing, combine the mayonnaise and lemon juice in a large bowl. In a separate bowl, combine the apples, celery and raisins. Sprinkle with lemon juice, salt and pepper. Toss with the dressing.

Before serving, toss the walnuts into the salad. Arrange lettuce leaves on large platter or individual salad plates. Place the salad atop the lettuce and serve.

Asian Cabbage Salad

A refreshing salad that works well with both Asian and non-Asian foods.

For the dressing:
1 cup (225 ml) rice vinegar
¼ cup (35 ml) vegetable oil
2 tbsp sesame oil
1–2 tbsp sugar

1 tbsp grated ginger
salt and pepper to taste

For the salad:
6 cups (450 g) shredded Chinese leaf (napa cabbage)
¼ cup (30 g) chopped fresh coriander (cilantro)

Combine the dressing ingredients and whisk together. Pour over the cabbage. Add cilantro, and mix well.

Greek Salad

For the salad:
1 head romaine lettuce, washed, dried and chopped or torn into bite-size pieces
1 small thinly sliced red onion
3 diced plum tomatoes
1 unpeeled English cucumber, coarsely chopped
½ cup (100 g) black olives, coarsely chopped (preferably Kalamata)
2 red or green peppers, seeded and chopped
1–2 cups (150–300 g) cherry or grape tomatoes, halved
½ tsp dried oregano
1 garlic clove, mashed or chopped into small pieces
¼ to ½ cup (50–100 g) feta cheese, crumbled or cut and drained into bite-size pieces

For the dressing:
3 tbsp extra virgin olive oil
1 tbsp lemon juice or red wine vinegar, or a mixture
1 or 2 chopped garlic cloves, if desired
½ tsp dried oregano
salt and pepper to taste

For the dressing, combine the vinegar with salt and pepper, garlic and oregano in a small bowl. Add the oil slowly in a thin stream while whisking. Continue to whisk thoroughly until blended. Once done, set aside.

In a large bowl, combine all the salad ingredients except the feta cheese. Toss with the dressing. Add the feta, and combine gently.

Serves 4 as a main dish

Scandinavian Cucumber Salad

A refreshing side salad.

For the salad:
3 large cucumbers
1 tbsp fresh chopped dill

For the dressing:
⅓ cup white wine vinegar
2 tbsp cider vinegar
1 tbsp sugar
2 tbsp water

Combine the vinegars, sugar and water. Stir until the sugar is dissolved. Set aside.

Slice the cucumbers in half lengthwise. Scoop out the seeds, and slice into thin rounds. Sprinkle with salt and allow to stand for an hour. Drain gently and pat dry.

Place the cucumbers in a large bowl and pour the vinegar mixture over them. Place on a large plate or bowl and sprinkle with dill.

Serves 4

Avocado, Onion and Tomato Salad

A salad without greens.

2 avocados, peeled and cut into bite-size pieces
½ medium size red onion
4 fresh tomatoes, cut in half vertically and sliced
1 tsp dried oregano or 1 tbsp chopped fresh oregano
¾ cup (165 ml) good-quality olive oil
¼ cup (55 ml) red wine vinegar

Place the sliced tomatoes on a large dish or serving platter. Drizzle olive oil and vinegar over them and sprinkle with oregano, salt and pepper. Cover and let sit for an hour outside the refrigerator.

Whisk the remainder of the oil and vinegar together until blended. Combine all the salad ingredients in a large bowl. Toss with the dressing. Add salt and pepper to taste. Top with fresh oregano, if using.

Serves 2 to 4

Raita with Shredded Cucumber

An Indian side-dish that can substitute for a more traditional salad.

2 cucumbers, peeled and shredded
2 cups Greek yoghurt
1 tbsp chopped fresh mint
½ tsp white sugar
salt and white pepper to taste

In a large bowl add the sugar, salt and pepper to the yoghurt. Let it sit in the refrigerator for one to two hours. Gently add the cucumber and mix to combine. Before serving, sprinkle with the chopped mint.

Serves 4 as a side-dish

Vietnamese Shredded Chicken Salad

This main-dish salad is easy to assemble.

For the salad:
1 store-bought rotisserie chicken
4 cups (300 g) shredded Chinese leaf (napa cabbage)
1 red bell pepper, seeds removed, sliced into bite-sized pieces
½ cup (60 g) chopped fresh mint
¼ cup (30 g) chopped fresh coriander (cilantro)
½ cup (70 g) chopped peanuts

For the dressing:
¼ cup (35 ml) fresh lime juice
3 tbsp vegetable oil
2 cloves minced garlic
2 tbsp sugar
2 tbsp Asian fish sauce

Skin and shred enough chicken to make 2 cups. In a large bowl, combine the cabbage and bell pepper. In a small bowl mix the dressing ingredients together. Pour dressing over the chicken and mix together with the cabbage and bell pepper. In a small bowl, combine mint and coriander, and add to the chicken mix. Sprinkle the peanuts over the mixture.

Serves 4

Bibliography

Albala, Ken, *The Banquet: Dining in the Great Courts of Late Renaissance Europe* (Urbana and Chicago, IL, 2007)
—, *Cooking in Europe, 1250–1650* (Westport, CT, and London, 2006)
—, *Eating Right in the Renaissance* (Berkeley, Los Angeles and London, 2002)
Bothwell, Don and Patricia, *Food in Antiquity* (London, 1969)
Capatti, Alberto, and Massimo Montanari, *Italian Cuisine: A Cultural History* (New York, 2003)
Caskey, Liz, *South American Cooking* (Guilford, CT, 2010)
Dalby, Andrew, *Food in the Ancient World from A to Z* (London and New York, 2003)
Ewing, Mrs Emma P., *Salad and Salad Making* (Chicago, IL, 1884)
Flandrin, Jean-Louis, *Arranging the Meal: A History of Table Service in France* (Berkeley, Los Angeles and London, 2007)
Glasse, Hannah, *The Art of Cookery Made Plain and Easy* (Carlisle, MA, 1998)
Grainger, Sally, and Christopher Grocock, *Apicius: A Critical Edition* (Totnes, 2006)
Grant, Mark, *Galen: On Food and Diet* (London and New York, 2000)
Guy, Christian, *An Illustrated History of French Cuisine*, trans. Elisabeth Abbott (New York, 1962)
Hulse, Olive M., *200 Recipes for Making Salads with Thirty Recipes for Dressing and Sauces* (Chicago, IL, 1910)

Ilkin, Nur, and Sheila Kaufman, *The Turkish Cookbook* (Northampton, 2010)

Maestro Martino of Como, *The Art of Cooking*, trans. and annot. Jeremy Parzen, ed. and intro. Luigi Ballerini (Berkeley and Los Angeles, CA, 2005)

Markham, Gervase, *The English Housewife* (Kingston and Montreal, 1986)

Marton, Beryl M., *The Complete Book of Salads* (New York, 1969)

Massonio, Salvatore, *Archidipno, overo Dell'insalate, e dell'uso di essa* (Venice, 1627)

May, Robert, *The Accomplisht Cook; or, The Art and Mystery of Cookery* (London, 1994)

Milham, Mary Ella, *Platina, On Right Pleasure and Good Health* (Tempe, AZ, 1998)

Miller, Gloria Bley, *The Thousand Recipe Chinese Cookbook* (New York, 1966)

Peterson, T. Sarah, *Acquired Taste: The French Origins of Modern Cooking* (Ithaca, NY, and London, 1994)

Rebora, Giovanni, trans. Albert Sonnenfeld, *Culture of the Fork* (New York, 1998)

Revel, Jean-François, *Culture and Cuisine: A Journey Through the History of Food* (New York, 1982)

Roden, Claudia, *The Food of Spain* (New York, 2011)

Rombauer, Irma S., *The Joy of Cooking* (New York, 1936)

Salads, including Appetizers: Favorite Recipes of Home Economics Teachers (Montgomery, AL, 1964), with acknowledgments to the American Dairy Association, Knox Gelatin, Inc., Kroger; Sunkist Growers, the USDA, Wesson Oil and Snowdrift People

Schlesinger, Chris, and John Willoughby, *Lettuce in Your Kitchen* (New York, 1996)

Scully, Terence, *The Art of Cookery in the Middle Ages* (Woodbridge, Suffolk, 1995)

—, *La Varenne's Cookery: François Pierre, Sieur de La Varenne* (Totnes, 2006)

—, *The Opera of Bartolomeo Scappi* [1570] (Toronto, Buffalo and London, 2008)

Shapiro, Laura, *Perfection Salad* (New York, 1986)

Shimizu, Shinko, *New Salads: Quick Healthy Recipes from Japan* (Tokyo, New York and San Francisco, 1986)

Toussaint-Samat, Maguelonne, *A History of Food*, trans. Anthea Bell (Oxford, 1992)

Tsuji, Shizuo, *Japanese Cooking: A Simple Art* (Tokyo, 1980)

Ude, Louis Eustache, *The French Cook* [1828] (New York, 1978)

Vehling, Joseph Dommers, *Apicius: Cooking and Dining in Imperial Rome* (New York, 1977)

Volokh, Anne, *The Art of Russian Cooking* (New York, 1983)

Weaver, William Woys, trans. and ed., *Sauer's Herbal Cures: America's First Book of Botanic Healing* (New York and London, 2001)

Wells, Patricia, *Salad as a Meal* (New York, 2011)

Wheaton, Barbara Ketcham, *Savoring the Past: The French Kitchen and Table from 1300 to 1789* (New York, 1983)

Acknowledgements

Thanks first of all should be given to Reaktion Books and publisher Michael R. Leaman who created this incomparable food history series. Thanks also to his excellent team at Reaktion and to the incomparable Andrew F. Smith, the editor of the series.

When I agreed to write the book, it hadn't occurred to me that although there are many salad cookbooks, the history of salad was a relatively new subject. That said, in his second-century *On the Powers of Food*, Galen of Pergamon got close when he identified and described individual foods of his time and how and when they were eaten. I am therefore indebted not only to Galen, but to the historian Mark Grant whose lucid description and English translation of Galen's work made it accessible.

For most of the rest of the material needed to investigate the subject, I am particularly grateful to the New York Public Library, which allowed me to assemble books in its Wertheim Study. It's one thing to read and take notes on a book, and another to be able to continue to refer to it. Thanks also go to my colleagues in food history Laura Shapiro, Anne Mendelson and Irene Sacks, to the friends who amazed me with their curiosity about the history of salad and to my children Claire Weinraub and Jesse Weinraub, who understandably had never given much thought to the subject but patiently listened to and were even interested in my discoveries.

Photo Acknowledgements

The author and the publishers wish to express their thanks to the below sources of illustrative material and/or permission to reproduce it:

Alamy: pp. 69 (Wayhunters), 96 (dbimages); Alka at SindhIRasoi. com: p. 72; Bigstock: pp. 71 (a003771), 92 (HandmadePictures); Boston Public Library: p. 84; Dreamstime: pp. 12 (Doethion), 23 (Rawlik), 36 (cobraphoto), 55 (Mirceaux), 88 (Helo80808); Foodista: p. 85; Getty Images: p. 31 (Leemage); iStockphoto: pp. 6 (Anthony Boulton), 10 (bhofack2), 14 (Night and Day Images), 15 (LOVE-LIFE), 16 (buccino tiphaine), 51 (MychkoAlezander), 52 (rez-art), 63 (modesigns58), 64 (DiyanaDimitrova), 75 (AdShooter), 90 (Lesyy), 93 (MarynaVoronova), 95 (luoman); Library of Congress, Washington, DC: p. 79; Mary Evans Picture Library: p. 37; The Metropolitan Museum of Art, New York: p. 21; © Musée du Louvre, Dist. RMN-Grand Palais/Art Resource, NY: p. 40; National Archives and Records Administration (NARA), Washington, DC: p. 94; REX Shutterstock: pp. 53 (Everett), 65 (imageBroker); Shutterstock: pp. 9 (Tamara Kulikova), 24 (Warren Price Photography), 41 (CKP1001), 58, 80 (gcpics), 83 (Carlos Yudica); Victoria & Albert Museum, London: p. 78; The Wellcome Library, London: pp. 34, 56; West Coast Seeds: p. 68.

Index

italic numbers refer to illustrations; **bold** to recipes